LANCA
MUR
CASEB

THIS BOOK SHOULD BE RETURNED ON OR BEFORE THE LATEST
DATE SHOWN TO THE LIBRARY FROM WHICH IT WAS BORROWED

X

AUTHOR	CLASS
FIELDING, S.	LR331

TITLE

Lancashire murder casebook

Other counties in this series
include

Essex
Shropshire
Sussex

LANCASHIRE
MURDER CASEBOOK

STEVE FIELDING

COUNTRYSIDE BOOKS
NEWBURY · BERKSHIRE

First published 1994
© Steve Fielding 1994

COUNTRYSIDE BOOKS
3 Catherine Road
Newbury, Berkshire

ISBN 1 85306 325 8

06376004

Produced through MRM Associates Ltd., Reading
Typeset by Paragon Typesetters, Queensferry, Clwyd
Printed by Woolnough Bookbinding, Irthlingborough

Acknowledgements

I would like to thank the following people: Lisa Moore, for her help in every stage of researching and writing the book. The staff in the Archives and Local Studies departments at the libraries in Bolton, Blackpool, Burnley, Morecambe, Rawtenstall, St Helens and the Wigan History Shop.

The following newspapers graciously gave permission to use photographs and illustrations from their libraries: *Bolton Evening News*, *Burnley Express*, *Lancashire Evening Post*, *Lancashire Evening Telegraph* and the *Morecambe Visitor*.

Thanks also to the following people who helped with the pictures and illustrations: John Lomas (Newspix), Peter G Reed (Preston), Brian White, Syd Dernley and Rachel at the Lancashire Evening Post library.

I have tried to contact all the copyright holders whose pictures appear in this book, but in one or two instances have been unable to trace their current whereabouts – I apologise in advance if I have inadvertently contravened any existing copyrights.

Contents

Introduction		8
1.	The Human Jigsaw	14
2.	A Domestic Tragedy	22
3.	Killer with a Wounded Thumb	25
4.	Death of a Nurse	29
5.	Footprints in the Flowerbeds	32
6.	The Locked Cabin	38
7.	The Body on the Beach	46
8.	'One of My Funny Moods'	50
9.	Hangman's Lament	56
10.	Murder on the Moors	62
11.	Revenge at the Wakes	66
12.	A Worthless Alibi	72
13.	Killer of Young Boys	81
14.	One Tell-Tale Sliver of Glass	86
15.	Mosaic of Murder	93
16.	The Good Samaritan	98
17.	Unwelcome Advances	103
18.	For Justice and Law	108
19.	The Vendetta	118

INTRODUCTION

Policing in Lancashire was once, as in many other regions, little more than a handful of parish constables working on a shoestring budget, relying in the main upon informers and monetary incentives to bring felons to justice. It was not until the beginning of the 19th century that the foundations of our modern police force first took root, when the London Metropolitan Police Force was founded in July 1829 by the then Home Secretary, Robert Peel.

Peel was a Lancastrian, born in Bury in 1788, and under his guidance the old style constables became 'peelers' or 'bobbies' and, sporting smart new uniforms, adhered to a strict code of law and order. In the next ten years, counties throughout the land followed London's lead and set up their own forces, both borough and rural.

In 1835, the Municipal Corporation Act recommended that any borough with a population over a certain number should organise its own police force, and in 1839, the Lancashire Borough Police Force was set up under the control of Captain Woodford. The initial strength was pro rata to the county population; the first roll call consisted of 500 Constables – about one to every 600 persons, 13 Superintendents and two Assistant Chief Constables.

In 1856, the County and Borough Police Act was passed, which obliged all towns to have their own police forces, and Captain Woodford, after inspecting the whole Lancashire force, suggested that a county force would serve the region better. It was not until 1969, over a hundred years later, that the county force was in fact created.

The success of any police force depends on public approval and support, and after a series of riots and disturbances in earlier years which were dealt with ruthlessly by the army, the public were initially a little wary of the new powers invested in the force. Officers had to work hard to gain the respect of those they served.

The region's standing as the hub of the Industrial Revolution brought with it problems associated with a heavily congested area.

Firstly the canals, then later the railways brought an influx of people seeking work, many travelling from other towns and cities in this county and from other parts of the United Kingdom, particularly Ireland. The region became the home of the first industrial society in the world, stretching all the way down from the Westmorland border to the river Mersey and eastwards to Oldham and Ashton.

The penalties that befell lawbreakers in Victorian times were strict and Lancashire boasted four main county gaols (at Kirkdale, Salford, Lancaster and Preston), as well as several smaller, rural ones. Prison cells were dank and the enforced labour back-breaking. A common form of punishment was transportation, firstly to America and later to Australia. This was often perilous and conditions on the overcrowded ships terrible. The convicts were shipped in cramped holds that were rife with disease, and many of those condemned to transportation died before the journey's end.

The third punishment widely used was hanging. There were over 200 offences that carried the death penalty at the time the police forces were being set up, and cases are recorded of children under ten years old being hanged for stealing a loaf of bread. Gradually as the force developed, then so too did various Parliamentary social reforms, and by 1861 the number of capital crimes was reduced to four.

In 1862, the first serving member of the Lancashire Constabulary was killed on duty. Two officers challenged a gang of men in Ashton-under-Lyne after a report of criminal damage at a brickworks. As the officers 'turned them over' (police slang for checking and searching), one of the gang drew a pistol and fired. Sergeant Harrap was hit in the head and chest but survived; Police Constable Jump was hit in the chest and died from his wounds. The gang fled, but officers searching the area found footprints in a number of bricks which were waiting to be fired up and when the suspects were arrested, prints of one of the men were found to be an exact match. The man who fired the shot was later hanged at Salford.

In 1867 a major incident occurred at Ardwick in Manchester. Two prominent members of a Fenian Nationalist Group were arrested in Manchester after a nationwide search. Known as 'Colonel Kelly' and 'Captain Deasey' the two were arrested on suspicion of burglary while loitering on a street corner. They resisted arrest and when detained were found to be carrying loaded guns. Although both had given false names to the arresting officer they were recognised back at the station. When it was learned that after an appearance in court

9

EXECUTION OF
ALLEN, GOULD, & LARKIN,

At the New Bailey Prison, Manchester, on Saturday, November 23rd, charged with the Wilful Murder of Sergeant Brett, at Manchester, on September 18th, 1867.

the authorities, who had erected barricades about every thirty yards, and so prevented the great pressure that would have been. The prisoners were astir at an early hour, and partook of the holy communion, and at the appointed time. Calcraft, the executioner, was introduced, when the operation of pinioning was gone through. The prisoners the meanwhile showed wonderful confidence, and appeared to be the least concerned. They all shook hands together and affectionately embraced one another, and declared themselves ready. The mournful procession was then formed, and at once proceeded towards the scaffold, where on their appearance there was a slight manifestation of applause. Everything having been prepared, the ropes adjusted, the signal was given, and the unhappy men were launched into eternity. The prisoners appeared to die very easy.

You true friends of liberty, and sons of the Emerald Isle,
Attend with an ear of sympathy to ... I now relate,
And to my sad story, I'd have you to list awhile,
Its of those poor unhappy men who now have met their fate;
Its Allen, Larkin, and Gould I mean, who of treason have been convicted,
Coupled with the crime of murder, for which we all deplore,
To the scaffold were condemned we see through struggling for
    liberty,
Of that poor unhappy country, the poor old shamrock shore.

Now its well known that Irishmen have oft upon the battle field,
Nobly fought our battles, against old England's foes.
And with the hearts of lions have forced her enemies to yield;
But to friends they are warm-hearted, as all the world well knows.
Its but for their rights they crave, old Ireland's honour for to save,
That has led to this calamity, for which we all deplore,
But by treachery they were betrayed, and these poor men have the
    forfeit paid,
And Allen, Gould, and Larkin, alas! are now no more.

It was at Manchester, as I now state, they sought their comrades
    to liberate,
And where is the man in such a state, would not have done the
    same?
Those poor men they were taken, for whom many hearts are aching,
For there is no one in reason their conduct can well blame
It was in the midst of that strife, that poor Brett lost his life,
That has caused the sons of Ireland most deeply to deplore,
And through that sad unhappy day, there's many a pitying heart
    will say,
Poor Allen, Gould, and Larkin, alas! are now no more.

These men they were convicted, and by the judge was sentenced,
And for murder and treason they were condemned to die,
And left to meet their fate to the gaze of all spectators,
Tho' that their lives would be spared it was the country's cry.
To God I recommend them, in his mercy to defend them,
May their souls shine in glory upon that blessed shore,
Safe within his keeping where there will be no weeping,
Now Allen, Gould, and Larkin, alas! are now no more.

This morning, Saturday, November 23rd, the three unfortunate convicts, Gould, Allen, and Larkin, suffered the extreme penalty of the law at the New Bailey prison, Manchester. Since their condemnation the culprits have behaved in a most exemplary manner, and have paid great attention to the Rev. gentlemen who attended them. They continued to declare their innocence to the last, and appeared to think themselves martyrs to a grand cause, and appeared quite ready for the event. The mob was very great, but not so large as it might have been, but for the precautions taken by

A broadsheet describing the death by hanging of three 'sons of the Emerald Isle'. The report says that 'The prisoners appeared to die very easy'.

10

they were to be taken to the Belle Vue gaol, the local Fenians plotted an ambush which was set for when the convoy reached Hyde Road, a mile or so from the prison. A large gang, led by William O'Meara Allen, attacked the convoy which was escorted by a dozen officers. The two men were held in a locked van by the resolute Sergeant, Charles Brett, who refused the attackers' repeated demands to release the prisoners.

Allen and his two lieutenants, William Gould and Michael Larkin, fired a volley of shots into the van, at which the Sergeant told them he had no intention of yielding to their demands, and he held firm until he made the mistake of putting his head near the ventilator grille to shout his defiance. As he did so a bullet from Allen's gun struck him in the head, killing him instantly. The three leaders were soon rounded up and after a short trial at Manchester Assizes they were hanged at the New Bailey Prison, Salford, in November 1867.

A policeman's pay was still poor in relation to many other occupations, and in 1888 Parliament created the County Councils which transferred control of the police from a magistrates committee to one comprising elected councillors and magistrates, known as a standing joint committee. One of the first bills passed by this committee was to bring the policeman's wage into line with that of a man working in industry and the position now paid a fair wage, if the hours worked – a seven day week was often the norm – still left something to be desired.

As with the world in general, the progress of time brought many new developments to the police force. In 1905 fingerprinting brought a useful aid in tracking criminals, and the great strides taken in the medical field all went to help solve cases. 1911 brought the first mounted police force, while the advent of the motor car was greatly appreciated by officers, as was radio technology that allowed officers to keep in touch without the outdated method of striking their truncheon on the pavement in a crude form of code.

Other developments included the training of detectives and formation of the CID; acceptance of women police officers; the formation of the fire brigade, which was another task taken away from the overworked bobby; and the use of police dogs which was implemented in the 1950s.

Although Lancashire cannot claim to have had the cream of the country's sensational murder cases during the 20th century, it could claim its fair share. One of the more infamous cases took place at Christmas 1919, when a young woman was found shot dead on the sandhills at St Anne's, near Blackpool. Skilful detective work soon had the killer in custody and a few months later he paid the full price for his crime.

The next Lancashire crime to grab the nation's attention was in the autumn of 1935 when the Buck Ruxton case hit the headlines. The story of Dr Ruxton opens this casebook on Lancashire Murders.

The Second World War brought thousands of conscripts into the area and the pressures and demands imposed upon a young soldier occasionally had tragic consequences, as the selection of wartime cases will testify. One famous Lancashire case from the immediate post-war years has been well documented elsewhere, but the execution of Walter Rowland in 1947 for the murder of a prostitute on a Manchester bomb-site, once again had crime reporters flocking to the area.

Rowland's execution was carried out by Albert Pierrepoint, who although a Yorkshireman by birth, had been brought up in Manchester and was the latest in a long line of Lancashire based hangmen. Since 1884, a Lancashireman had been the country's chief executioner and this carried on until 1964 when Harry Allen and Leslie Stewart, both residents of the county, carried out the last death sentences in Great Britain.

The selection of cases from the 1950s, while they cannot be said to be sensational, are certainly typical crimes of the day, and the cases that close the book are a mixed bag of depravity, greed and revenge.

All the early cases included in this casebook were investigated by the Lancashire Constabulary, often overseeing the local town force, but in April 1969, despite some opposition, the town and borough forces were amalgamated into the county force. Salford merged with Manchester, Bootle with Liverpool, and all others with Lancashire which became one of the biggest forces in the country. Just as officers had become used to the new structure there was another change.

On Monday, 1st April, 1974, the recommendation of the Boundaries Commission implemented a radical re-writing of the county borders, and in doing so gave rise to three new counties in what was the old Lancashire county. Henceforth, some former Lancastrians found themselves living in Merseyside, Greater Manchester and Cumbria.

The police force was also seriously affected by these changes, and in one fell swoop the strength of the Lancashire Police Force was cut from almost 7,000 serving officers, to less than 3,000 strong.

Today, aided by new technology, the force has gone from strength to strength, but it is a testament to the pioneering skills of the early detectives that the high success rate in dealing with major crime has altered very little since the early days of the Lancashire Constabulary.

Steve Fielding
Autumn 1994

1

THE HUMAN JIGSAW

**THE MURDERS OF MARY ROGERSON AND ISABELLA RUXTON
AT LANCASTER, SEPTEMBER 1935**

On Tuesday, 1st October, 1935, police in Lancaster received a visit from Mrs Jessie Rogerson. She was concerned about her 20 year old stepdaughter, Mary, who worked as a live-in housemaid to a local doctor and had not been seen for several days by her parents, although they usually kept in touch almost daily. Mrs Rogerson told police that she had visited Dr Ruxton's surgery on 25th September, when the doctor told her Mary had gone to Edinburgh with his wife, who was nursing Mary after she had had her pregnancy terminated. That was over a week ago, and the story didn't ring true at all to the worried stepmother. Mrs Rogerson had told Dr Ruxton that if Mary wasn't home by the weekend, they would go to the police.

Dr Buck Ruxton was already known to the Lancaster police. Ruxton was the assumed name of Bukhtyar Rustomji Ratnji Hakim, a Parsee, born to respectable, well-to-do parents in Bombay in 1899. A graduate from Bombay University, he had worked in a number of European cities before originally settling in Edinburgh. There he became friendly with a large circle of Edinburgh's more affluent citizens, who took to the dashing, handsome Parsee, and he fell in love with an attractive divorcee, Isabella Van Ess, who since the separation from her Dutch husband had been working as a manageress in a city centre restaurant.

Ruxton, a neurotic, highly volatile young man, seemed to have found his equal in Isabella and after a stormy, tempestuous courtship they had moved in together as man and wife. In the spring of 1930, now the doting father of a baby daughter, he brought his family to Lancaster where he took over a surgery at 2 Dalton Square. He threw

Ruxton's surgery in Lancaster. *(Lancashire Evening Post)*

himself into the new practice and quickly became a well respected local doctor. His family increased with the birth of another daughter.

Ruxton and Isabella's domestic lifestyle was fraught with fights and separations and had brought him to the attention of the police. By early 1934, Ruxton was frequently resorting to violence against his wife, accusing her of having an affair or of flirting with their friends, although he was always quick to beg her forgiveness when he calmed down. 'We are the kind of people who cannot live with each other and cannot live without each other', he was fond of saying, and on more than one occasion Isabella had reported him to the police after

15

he had made threats to kill her. Then they employed a young housekeeper, Mary Jane Rogerson, to look after the children, and her presence had seemed to diffuse the tension in the house for a time.

When detectives paid Dr Ruxton a visit following Mrs Rogerson's report of her concern, he confirmed that his wife and maid had gone away for a while. There was nothing unduly suspicious in his statement, and satisfied for the moment that the doctor was telling the truth, the officers left. They made a few enquiries and found that Isabella had visited her sister in Blackpool on 14th September. This was the last time she was seen alive.

Reports of the disappearance of Mary Rogerson appeared in several newspapers, including the *Daily Record*, a copy of which was read by the Chief Constable of Dumfries, who had his own mystery to solve.

On the warm Sunday afternoon of 29th September a young Edinburgh holidaymaker had made a gruesome discovery at Moffat, a small town north of Dumfries on the Edinburgh road. Reaching a small bridge crossing Gardenholm Linn, a tributary of the river Annan, she had paused to take in the autumn air, and looking down into the gully spotted what looked like a human arm, wrapped in newspaper, trapped between boulders in the fast flowing waters.

The subsequent police search continued throughout the day and over 70 body parts were gathered up along the riverbank and later transferred to a local hospital. Baffled by the maggot-ridden, decomposing flesh, officers called in Edinburgh-based Professor John Glaister and Doctor Gilbert Miller to assist in identifying the human jigsaw. Professor Glaister was soon able to tell detectives that whoever was responsible for dismembering the bodies possessed a detailed anatomical knowledge, and almost all traces of identification, such as teeth and eyes, had been removed. He also told police that their initial estimate of half a dozen bodies was way out, and in fact the limbs came from just two bodies, one male and one female. Next morning he changed his opinion to that of two females; one aged around 40, the other perhaps half that age.

Officers from Glasgow CID joined in the investigation. No local people were reported missing and investigations into anything suspicious seen on the roads around Moffat in the previous week also drew a blank.

While Professor Glaister and his team worked on identifying the bodies, police officers concentrated their efforts on the newspapers that the limbs were wrapped in. They were found to come from an edition of the *Sunday Graphic*, a nationally distributed newspaper, but

Mrs Isabella Ruxton. *(Lancashire Evening Post)*

the pages that contained the limbs revealed an important clue. One of the sheets contained the heading '. . . AMBE'S CARNIVAL QUEEN – CROWNED'. Dated 15th September, the heading came from a 'slip edition' of the *Sunday Graphic* only available in Morecambe, Lancaster and the immediate area. There would have been less than 4,000 copies of this edition printed. This narrowed down the investigating area, but they still needed to check on all inhabitants, which wasn't easy as the region was a popular holiday destination. Then reports of the disappearance of Mary Rogerson and Isabella Ruxton began to appear.

Things now moved at a pace. Police returned to the doctor's surgery and re-interviewed Ruxton, while other detectives questioned members of his staff and neighbours. Again they couldn't

Buck Ruxton. *(Lancashire Evening Post)*

find anything against the doctor other than suspicion, an undoubted anatomical knowledge and a missing wife. Two days later Ruxton stormed into Lancaster police station, demanding to speak to Captain Vann, the Chief Constable.

'Can't you publish it in the papers that there is no connection between the bodies found in Scotland and the disappearance of my wife?' he pleaded. Captain Vann studied him calmly and said that if and when he was satisfied that Ruxton wasn't involved, then he would consider his request.

Twenty-four hours later the police had the breakthrough they needed. Detectives checking on a number of items of clothing found in the stream had at last found conclusive proof linking them to the missing women. One item, a blouse, had been repaired with a makeshift patch and Mrs Rogerson confirmed that the repair was her own handiwork, even showing officers the material from which the patch had been cut.

On 13th October, 1935, Dr Buck Ruxton was arrested on suspicion of murdering his wife and housemaid and on the following day detectives converged on Ruxton's house and went over every inch. There was an odd yellow sheen on the bath which a pathologist was able to confirm was dried blood. It appeared that the dissection of the bodies had taken place in the bath and further examination found blood under the adjacent floorboards, confirming the theory. Later that afternoon Ruxton was formally charged with murder.

When Dr Ruxton stood trial at Manchester Assizes before Mr Justice Singleton in March 1936, he had in his corner a formidable counsel led by the great Norman Birkett KC. Ruxton was to be the only witness called for the defence. He faced an almost overwhelming case built up by the prosecution. The reason for the murders, the prosecution maintained, was simple. During one of their frequent and violent rows, he had killed Isabella as he had so often threatened to do, probably by strangulation. Young Mary had stumbled in on him, and he had to silence her. He had carefully dismembered the bodies and disposed of them far from Lancaster, but in an area he knew well.

Ruxton's confession.

19

The official notices are posted after Ruxton's execution. *(Lancashire Evening Post)*

When Ruxton took his place in the dock, the formerly personable doctor made a pitiful showing. Frequently in tears, he strenuously denied all charges and in replying to the charge that he murdered his housemaid he replied, 'It is absolute bunkum with a capital B, if I may say so. Why should I kill young Mary?'

The trial lasted eleven days and ended when the all male jury took just one hour to find him guilty. He appealed against the sentence but at a hearing before the Lord Chief Justice the appeal was dismissed, and on Tuesday, 12th May, 1936, Dr Buck Ruxton was hanged at Strangeways prison, Manchester.

On the following Sunday a note confessing the murder appeared in the *News of the World*:

Lancaster
14.10.35

I killed Mrs Ruxton in a fit of temper because I thought she had been with a man. I was Mad at the time. Mary Rogerson was present at the time. I had to kill her.

B. Ruxton

The remarkable thing about the confession was that it was dated the day after his arrest and had been given to a journalist for a fee of £3,000. The money was later used to pay his defence costs, which explained why he was able to engage the most eminent defence counsel of the day. It had been in a sealed envelope only to be opened after Ruxton's death.

2

A DOMESTIC TRAGEDY

THE MURDER OF ELIZA CALDWELL AT ROCHDALE, FEBRUARY 1938

The Depression of the 1930s brought hardship and tragedy to many households, but none more so than that of Charlie and Eliza Caldwell, who had fallen in love during the equally dark days of the First World War.

It was while interred in Switzerland awaiting repatriation from a German prisoner of war camp that Charlie met pretty Eliza Augustine. The relationship blossomed and when hostilities ended in the autumn of 1918, they married at Montreux before returning to live in England.

They chose to settle in Charlie's home town of Rochdale and in the immediate post-war years their family grew, first with a son and two years later a daughter. As the country readjusted to the aftermath of war, the Caldwell family lived happily enough together.

Charlie had always found steady skilled work in the local mills, but by the mid 1930s he was out of work and taking on anything he could turn his hand to, including hawking and rag collecting. Eliza managed to find herself a job as a seamstress, so there was some money coming into the house, but Charlie increasingly drowned his sorrows in drink. The seeds had been sown for a tragedy that would tear the family apart.

As the new year of 1938 dawned, the couple greeted it as they had seen out the old year, by fighting with each other. Eventually Eliza had had enough. One morning in February, tired of the constant rowing, she took their daughter and a few belongings and headed for the sanctuary of a workmate, Jane Lee's home. Eliza wanted space and time to consult a solicitor regarding a separation order. Their son, who had started a job in January, had also left to find lodgings of his own. Charlie was left to fend for himself.

The day after leaving her husband, Eliza called back at the house on Clementina Street to collect some more of her belongings and found she was unable to gain entry. She hailed a passing policeman and, explaining the situation, got him to force the door open. To her horror she found that the contents of the living room had been smashed up and stacked high in a pile in the centre of the room, as if ready for a bonfire.

Charlie was in another room, drunk, and the police officer had to forcibly restrain Eliza from striking him. After reassurances from both parties that there would be no more trouble the constable left.

Eliza collected the clothes and told Charlie she would call in the next day to see him. Charlie asked where she was staying but she refused to tell him. However, he called on his son later that day and after convincing the lad that he wanted to try and save his marriage, Charlie got him to reveal her whereabouts.

On the afternoon of 11th February, Charlie and his son waited at a bus stop on Halifax Road for Eliza to arrive home from work. They watched as she alighted from the trolley bus and followed her up the road. Charlie began pleading with her to come home, but it was to no avail. As they reached the corner, Eliza turned round and yelled, 'I'm not coming home!'

In an instant Charlie pulled out a dagger and plunged it deep into her chest. Eliza staggered into a local butcher's shop and collapsed against the counter. She was dead before help could be summoned. Charlie made a half-hearted attempt to escape but was taken to Rochdale police station.

After being questioned for a long period, he was left unattended for a moment to collect his thoughts. Although the murder weapon had been taken from him, Charlie had concealed another knife in his clothing. A constable re-entered the room just in time to see him raise the knife he held in his hand and attempt to cut his own throat. The officer rushed across the room and dashed the blade from his grasp.

In tears Charlie told him, 'I wouldn't have killed my wife if that woman hadn't come between us.' He then made a statement and was remanded in custody.

When Charlie Caldwell stood trial before Mr Justice Hucker at Manchester Assizes on 14th March, 1938, the defence counsel claimed that Eliza's workmate, the unfortunate Mrs Lee, had deliberately come between husband and wife, convincing Eliza she would be better off away from her husband. For the prosecution, it was a simple case of murder; Caldwell had killed his wife because she had rejected him.

The trial lasted one day and ended with Mr Justice Hucker pronouncing the death sentence. Against Charlie's wishes an appeal was made on the prisoner's behalf, but it was rejected.

Forty year old Charlie Caldwell continued to tell the guards in the condemned cell at Strangeways prison that he didn't want a reprieve and that he wanted the rope. On Wednesday morning, 20th April, 1938, he got his wish.

3

KILLER WITH A WOUNDED THUMB

THE MURDER OF MARY HAGAN AT LIVERPOOL, NOVEMBER 1940

'Come on, Mary, you'd better be sharp if you're going to fetch the paper,' James Hagan told his daughter as he looked at the clock on the mantelpiece. It was 6.30 pm, Saturday evening, 2nd November, 1940, and in 15 minutes the shutters on the newsagent's would be down and he would have to do without his cigarettes and *Liverpool Echo*.

Fifteen year old Mary was a sensible, well behaved young lady, and although the blacked-out streets were shrouded in darkness, James Hagan hardly gave a second thought about sending her to the shop. With the two shillings in her hand, Mary left her home on Brookside Avenue, in the Waterloo district of Liverpool and set out for the shop on nearby Sandy Lane. She never returned.

Two hours later her worried parents contacted the local police. Constable Dixon was sent to the house and it was decided to form a search party. Friends and neighbours offered to help and split into pairs, with each taking a specific area.

One of the search parties, led by the local ARP warden, took the area at the end of Brook Vale, where Mary would have passed on her way to the shop. At the point where Brook Vale merged with Cambridge Road and Sandy Lane, the road crossed over the Waterloo to Lime Street railway line, and against the bridge was a concrete blockhouse used by the Home Guard as an anti-invasion fortress.

In the almost total darkness they shone their torches into the dank, soot-stained building. The warden waded through an ankle-deep, stagnant puddle of water, the remnants of a recent downpour, and shining the light towards the far corner, he picked out the shape of a figure lying on a mound of earth. He had found Mary Hagan.

Mary had been raped and then strangled. She had bruises on her face and her clothing was torn and dishevelled. She had died at about 7 pm. On the floor beside her was the copy of the *Echo* her father had sent her out to get, but there was no sign of the cigarettes or change.

Detective Chief Superintendent Jackson of Liverpool CID took charge of the investigation and under electric arc lights he and his officers searched for clues. Unfortunately, the discovery of Mary's body had caused dozens of the searchers to converge on the blockhouse and as a result any footprints the killer may have left in his wake had been obliterated.

In the blockhouse itself, however, beside the body was a clear impression of a boot heel, and a cast was made. The floor was covered in dead leaves blown in from the nearby field, sweet wrappers, cigarette butts and spent matches, mostly floating in a large pool of water, which was cleared with a stirrup pump. Anything dragged up was placed on blotting paper and examined in minute detail. Jackson thought he had unearthed a good clue when a handkerchief marked 'G Rimmer' was found near the body, but despite extensive enquiries no 'G Rimmer' from the area, and there were several, could be linked with the crime.

The search for clues at the blockhouse did yield a significant discovery. It was found that Mary had eaten a bar of chocolate shortly before her death and amongst the debris removed from the puddle was a chocolate wrapper which matched a tiny piece found on Mary's clothing. The wrapper found on the floor was examined under a microscope and found to have traces of zinc ointment and antiseptic. Also recovered from the water was a stained bandage, shaped as if to protect a thumb wound. Dr Firth, head of the Home Office forensic laboratory at Preston, confirmed that the bandage was part of an Army field dressing, and the fact that it had been treated, unnecessarily, with the zinc ointment suggested that it was not administered by a medical orderly. The traces of ointment on the wrapper proved that the wearer of the bandage had come into contact with Mary and so, the detectives reasoned, if they could find the owner of the bandage, then they would also have found the killer. However, with literally thousands of troops stationed in wartime Lancashire this was going to be no easy task.

A radio appeal was made for anyone who had seen Mary before

7 pm, or had seen anyone acting suspiciously in the locality. Several witnesses reported seeing a young soldier with an East Lancashire accent and a cut face. A woman told detectives that a soldier with a cut on his face had approached her as she entered her front door and asked to use her bathroom to clean up. He said that he had been involved in a fight with another soldier, but being alone in the house at the time she refused him entry and watched from the window as he walked away.

The appeal also brought police information on an earlier crime a mile or so from the scene of Mary's murder. A month before, on 4th October, a cyclist named Anne McVitte had been attacked and robbed by a young soldier as she pedalled along a canal bank. She had avoided further attack by jumping into the water and swimming across to the other side. The man had stolen her purse containing just under £2, and her bicycle. Other witnesses had reported seeing a soldier near the canal bank shortly before the attack. The descriptions of the soldiers in both these cases sounded uncannily similar.

Seventeen days after the murder, a telephone call sent detectives rushing down to London to interview a soldier being held at Streatham in connection with the assault on Anne McVitte. Twenty-eight year old Samuel Morgan was a member of the Irish Guards and lived at Berkeley Drive, Seaforth, which bordered with Waterloo in the north west corner of Liverpool. He had a freshly healed scar on his right thumb. Chief Superintendent Jackson arranged for Morgan to be brought to Liverpool for questioning.

A search was made of Morgan's mother's house and officers found a piece of field dressing, being used as a face cloth, in the bathroom. A piece had been snipped from the corner and when checked it was found to match the bandage discovered at the murder scene. The stitching was also examined under microscope and it was found that this particular piece of bandage had been 'double stitched' as opposed to the standard single stitch. The chances of the bandage coming from any piece of dressing other than the one found in Morgan's bathroom were thousands to one. To back this up officers collected together scores of field dressings from units throughout the north west and no other one had double stitching. It was the breakthrough the police needed.

A number of witnesses identified Morgan as the soldier seen near the scene of the crime shortly before the murder and the landlord of a local pub reported seeing Morgan in his bar at 7.45 pm that night. He had had a bloodstain on his cap and was bleeding from a wound to his hand. Another person from the public house claimed that he had helped refasten the bandage earlier in the evening and when he saw Morgan later that night the bandage was missing. Morgan's boots were removed and checked against the plaster cast made from beside the body. A perfect match.

On Monday, 17th February 1941, Samuel Morgan stood in the dock at Liverpool Assizes. Faced with a wealth of evidence that he had been with the dead girl, Morgan conceded that he had robbed Mary of some cigarettes and a few pennies but denied rape and murder. It was no surprise when the jury took only a short time to return a guilty verdict. Morgan, dressed in his best uniform, stood smartly to attention as sentence of death was passed on him.

On Friday morning, 4th April, Samuel Morgan was hanged at Walton prison. He made no confession but the strength of the police evidence against him left no one in any doubt that when the trapdoor opened beneath Morgan's feet, justice had been done for Mary Hagan.

4

DEATH OF A NURSE

THE MURDER OF IMELDRED OSLIFF AT SOUTHPORT, FEBRUARY 1942

If one thing could be said about Douglas Edmundson it was that he had an eye for a pretty girl, and unfortunately for them a lot of pretty girls had an eye for him.

Amongst the many ladies Edmundson courted was 28 year old Imeldred Maria Osliff who lived with her parents on Moss Lane, Banks, Southport. She had known Edmundson since school and was so infatuated with him that on the promise of marriage they became lovers, and although her parents had never met the young man she frequently referred to him as her fiancé.

The outbreak of the Second World War saw the 25 year old leave his native Southport to become a petty officer in the Navy. He served as a stoker on several ships and while aboard the carrier *Ark Royal* in the spring of 1941, he was seriously injured after being caught up in an intensive, sustained attack on the ship which left him with a slight limp and damaged arm.

In June 1941, while recuperating at Evesham hospital in the Midlands, he met Delia Chatterton. Although both were engaged, their respective partners were elsewhere and they were instantly attracted to each other, the young nurse in particular being struck on the dashing sailor. They soon fell in love and on his discharge from hospital they travelled to his camp at Devonport and married.

Edmundson and his wife were happy enough, but although she received money from a naval trust and had a job with the Government, he still found himself short of cash. In January 1942, only a few months after his marriage, Edmundson returned to Southport and had no hesitation in contacting Imeldred by letter begging for her help. He had neglected to inform her of his marriage, but word had reached her. Although angered and upset, she agreed to meet him.

Imeldred had worked as a children's nurse in the Civil Nursing Reserve at Southport hospital for 18 months, but in the winter of 1941 she had transferred to the isolation ward at New Hall, Birkdale, an annexe of the main Southport hospital. She left home at 11 am on Saturday, 7th February to go on duty and walked with her father to the bus stop, telling him that she would not be home for tea as she was meeting Douglas, her fiancé, and they were going to the theatre. She finished her shift in the early evening and left the hospital with another nurse. That was the last time she was seen alive.

Imeldred met Edmundson in Victoria Park, Southport that evening. What did she expect when she met her lover again? Whatever her intentions, it all went horribly wrong. According to Edmundson, she told him that she was prepared to lend him some money, but when he said that it was not only for himself but also for his wife, she became abusive and refused him the money. Imeldred, he said, had tried to break up his marriage by writing to his wife's parents informing them that he had promised to marry her, but it was only when she began to insult his wife that he lost his temper and grabbed her by the throat.

Early next morning, a man out walking his dog on Victoria Park found a woman's body lying in the bushes close to the entrance. Her clothing had been torn and she had evidently been strangled. Her handbag and purse which contained her identity card was missing, but later that afternoon Frederick Osliff was able to confirm to police that the body was that of his daughter, Imeldred.

The investigation was handled by Detective Inspector Mighall and Detective Sergeant Cook, and from the grieving parents they learned of Imeldred's assignation on the previous evening with her fiancé. Who was this Douglas Edmundson? Her parents somewhat shame-fully admitted knowing nothing about him, but enquiries soon brought some important information. It was learned that Imeldred had last been seen at around 9 pm with her fiancé, and a short time later a man matching his description boarded a train for Liverpool carrying a small black bag. Later that Sunday afternoon, police in Liverpool found the bag, which proved to have belonged to the murdered nurse, in Church Street, close to the YMCA.

The hunt for Petty Officer Edmundson was only a short one. He was known to have friends at Evesham and from them it was learned he had travelled to Birmingham, where early on Tuesday morning he was taken into custody.

On Monday, 20th April, 1942, Douglas Edmundson stood trial for murder at Liverpool Assizes, before Mr Justice Wrottesley. He pleaded not guilty. Evidence was given that on several occasions Edmundson had written to Imeldred asking for help and that she had eventually given in to his request. They had arranged to meet and he then made 'a desperate attempt for monetary assistance'. While in the park he strangled her and stole her bag, which contained money and letters she carried written by him.

The trial lasted two days, and on the last day the defence realised their only hope rested in proving that Edmundson was insane. His wife took the stand and testified that her husband lived in a semi-fantasy world and had a tendency to 'sheer romance'. During their marriage he had told her more than one incredible tale: once that he was to be posted overseas to Africa, and it was only after he had bought and packed a number of cases did she find out that it was all a lie, and on another occasion he came home and told her that his brother Norman had been killed in an air crash while serving in the RAF, which again was untrue. Why should he say and do these things, his defence suggested, if he wasn't suffering from some form of insanity? The jury was unconvinced, and on 24th June, 1942, Douglas Edmundson was hanged at Walton prison for the murder of the woman who loved him.

5
FOOTPRINTS IN THE FLOWERBEDS

THE MURDER OF GLADYS APPLETON AT ST HELENS, MARCH 1944

It started out as just another day for postwoman Betsy Baines as she began her round early on Monday morning, 20th March. At 7.45 am, Betsy turned into Cowley Hill Lane, St Helens, and what she discovered next started off a major murder enquiry. Walking back down the drive after delivering letters at The Elms, a detached house used since the outbreak of the war as the headquarters of the National Fire Service, she spotted the body of a young woman lying in the bushes.

It appeared the woman had been the victim of a brutal sex attack. Her clothes had been savagely ripped, exposing the whole of her body, and there was a clear set of teeth marks on and around her breasts. The cause of death though, was clearly strangulation; a scarf was knotted tightly around the neck with the two ends forced inside her mouth.

Superintendent James Ball and Detective Inspector John Maddocks took charge of the investigation. From the woman's handbag found nearby, papers revealed her to be 27 year old Gladys May Appleton of Bishop Road, St Helens. Detectives interviewed her distressed parents and Frederick Appleton confirmed that the body was indeed that of his daughter. He told Superintendent Ball that she had failed to return home the night before after visiting her boyfriend, George Barker.

Barker had been courting Gladys since soon after the outbreak of the war, some four years ago. They usually went for a drink on Sundays but they had spent the previous evening in together, as he was still feeling the effects of a visit to the dentist. He lived on

32

The Elms.

Knowlesly Road, a quarter of an hour's walk from Gladys's home, and would normally have walked her to her door, but on this night she said she would be all right walking home alone and they had parted at his front door at 10.40 pm. It was a decision that would haunt George Barker for the rest of his life.

Several local witnesses mentioned seeing a soldier in the Cowley Hill Lane area at around the time Gladys had left Barker's house. Two things they all agreed on; that he spoke with a strong Scottish accent and that he was very drunk.

Martha Leigh told police that she was walking up Windle Street towards her front door, when she heard a woman scream.

'It was a terrible scream,' she told the officer, 'and it seemed to die down into a smothered groan. It was a few minutes after eleven o'clock.'

Arthur Jenkins was walking home with his wife at 11.15 pm when he heard footsteps and saw the figure of a soldier approaching. He asked to be directed to the Capitol Theatre and they showed him the way. Jenkins said that the man seemed agitated and out of breath. Witness Ronald Meyer also told detectives that he had been stopped by a soldier and asked where a certain hotel was. The soldier had told him that he had missed his last bus. Meyer had suggested the YMCA but the soldier told him they were full. He was asked if the Capitol Theatre was open, and Meyer said that there would probably be a fire-watcher on duty. Investigations showed that the soldier had been allowed shelter in the stalls and after a night's sleep he had left at first light.

The police were faced with the task of finding one amongst the thousands of servicemen who had been drafted into the area. It would take exhaustive enquiries to check on the whereabouts of them all, but it was a task that had to be done and a team of officers drew up a list of all camps within an hour of St Helens. Detectives from Scotland Yard were asked to give assistance and the investigation was put into the hands of Detective Inspector Philpott and Detective Sergeant McGinn.

Then another witness gave them the help they desperately needed. Mrs Gene Galvin of Gamble Avenue told officers that she was making her way home at around 10.30 pm when she was confronted by a young Scottish soldier. He told her that he had just come from The Rifles, a local public house, and although she had quickened her step he kept up with her, chatting until they reached her front gate.

He told her that 'he would love to be going home to a nice soft bed', and she suggested that if he found himself a private billet then he would have a soft bed. Bidding him goodnight, she opened the gate, closed it directly behind her, and walked up the drive. The soldier opened the gate and followed her up. He told her he would walk her to the front door and kiss her goodnight. She said that he was mistaken and hurried up the drive, but the youth followed her and said that he couldn't understand English girls. She asked him again to leave and he said he wouldn't go until he had kissed her goodnight, even if it meant waiting all night.

Becoming worried, she jumped onto the lawn and he ran after her, leaving a trail of footprints in the flower beds. Gene reached the house and pounded on the door shouting for her mother. The noise was enough to frighten him off and he fled down the drive. It was a lucky escape. She was able to give officers a good description of him: fresh faced, probably around 18 years old, fair haired, average height, slimly built and with a Scottish accent.

The footprints could still be clearly seen in the earth and on Wednesday morning, Chief Inspector Duncan, in charge of finger-prints and photography at the Lancashire police headquarters, visited the scene and took a number of photographs of the footprints as well as making several plaster casts. It seemed unlikely that there had been two drunken young Scotsmen in the area at the same time, and beyond doubt that half an hour after Gene Galvin's encounter, Gladys Appleton had met her death in similar circumstances.

It now became a manhunt. Detectives had several independent witnesses whose testimonies all verified each other. They had a good description of the wanted man and casts of his footprints. The process of elimination had begun almost at once but it was, as expected, a painfully slow one, and it was to be twelve days before the murderer was in custody.

On Friday, 31st March Detective Inspector Maddocks received a call from a nearby military camp, and was told that a young soldier arrested for being absent without leave fitted the description of the St Helens murderer. Later that morning officers questioned John Gordon Davidson, who was being held in a detention cell at the camp.

John Gordon Davidson was 18 years old, away from his home in Grangemouth, Stirlingshire for the first time and stationed at a camp near St Helens, one of thousands of young servicemen awaiting whatever the war might bring in 1944. On 19th March, after an evening of heavy drinking with two fellow soldiers in The Rifles pub in St Helens, he went out alone looking for a woman.

Davidson told them that he had been in a public house with two women until 10.30 pm, when he left them to catch a bus back to camp. He had missed the bus and spent the night in the stalls at a nearby cinema. He was questioned about accosting a woman in Gamble Avenue and he denied it at first, but later admitted that he had tried to kiss her. He just 'didn't want to get mixed up in the murder'.

An examination was made of Davidson's kit-bag and several items, including a pair of his shoes, were taken away for further examination at the forensic department at Preston. He was taken to St Helens police station, where he steadfastly maintained his innocence until, with midnight approaching, he suddenly put his head in his hands and began to cry.

Detective Sergeant Frank McGinn asked him what was the matter?

'I did it,' he replied. 'I did it to that poor girl. What made me do it? How will I die? Let me tell you all about it.'

Superintendent Ball was sent for and in his presence Davidson dictated a statement.

Gladys May Appleton. *(St Helens Archives and Local Studies)*

'I was in St Helens on March 19, Sunday. I was with Lance Corporal Green and Private Sanderson in The Rifles with two young girls and an old woman. I left them and met a woman and took her home to her gate. She would not let me kiss her. I ran after her, and she went into the house. I came away, and started to walk and met the girl. I asked her to walk to the Capitol. I took her in the gate. I kissed her. She didn't like it. I choked her with my hands. She struggled, and I put her on the grass, and I killed her there. I just choked her. I tore her clothes and tried . . . ' Tears filled his eyes as he continued. 'I ran away and went to the Theatre and stayed there until morning. Then I went back to the camp. It was about 6.30 am. I have been worrying all the time.'

36

When charged with murder he wept freely and replied, 'I didn't mean to do it.'

On the following morning, at a hastily convened session of the Borough Police Court, Davidson was remanded for a further week. Standing in his khaki uniform, he looked a broken man. His eyes were inflamed from constant crying and he hung his head in shame throughout the proceedings. Sobbing uncontrollably, the young soldier was escorted from the proceedings and taken to Walton prison.

Davidson was committed for trial at Manchester Assizes, and on Monday 2nd May, he found himself before Mr Justice Hilberry. His appearance mirrored that of when he was remanded. Sobbing quietly, he replied 'Not Guilty' to the charges and his head weighed heavily against his chest as the prosecution put its case. Mr Kenneth Burke, his vastly experienced defence counsel, could do little.

The judge's summing up, which lasted for just under an hour, invited the jury to consider all the evidence they had heard. He pointed out that the prosecution's case was a strong one but it was left to them to decide if it was proved beyond doubt that Davidson was guilty, that those footprints in the flowerbed were also those of Gladys Appleton's murderer. They needed just 34 minutes to find him guilty but added a strong recommendation for mercy on account of his youth.

Davidson stood smartly to attention as sentence of death was pronounced and was then led sobbing bitterly from the dock. An appeal was launched but met with no success. He penned a farewell letter to his foster mother in which he blamed his position on drink, and said that he prayed the war would be over before his young stepbrother was old enough to be called up.

On Wednesday, 12th July, he was hanged at Walton prison, sobbing gently as the hangman placed the noose around his neck.

It was a sad conclusion to a sad case; a homesick young soldier fuelled with drink gave way to sexual frustration and paid the ultimate price for his crime, and a blameless young woman lost her life.

6

THE LOCKED CABIN

THE MURDER OF JAMES PERCEY AT SALFORD, APRIL 1944

The journey through the waters of the North Atlantic had been treacherous. The silent enemy below – the German U-boats – saw to that, but as the merchant vessel *Pacific Shipper* edged its way slowly into the mouth of the river Mersey, the crew began to relax, ready for a spot of well earned shore leave. It was Saturday, 1st April 1944.

Safely in Salford Docks most of the crew headed for town, leaving just a skeleton staff to watch over the ship. Apart from basic security, their only task was to adhere to the strict blackout regulations. At shortly before 11 pm on the following Saturday night, 8th April, the third mate was doing a routine security check when he spotted a chink of light coming from the second officer's cabin.

'Hey! Put that bloody light out,' he barked, bounding up the stairs. Reaching the bridge he was on the point of repeating his command when he became aware of a strange smell evidently coming from the chief's cabin, situated inside the second officer's cabin and accessible only by passing through it. He tried the door but it was locked. Switching off the light he returned to his patrol and thought no more about it until an hour or so later when he entered the officers' lavatory directly below the locked cabin. His gaze was attracted to a dark patch on the ceiling that looked uncannily like blood. Realising what was directly above, and remembering the smell, he quickly sought out the first mate who kept keys to all the cabins. The first mate was ashore but the keys were hanging on the wall, and selecting the appropriate bunch he returned to the bridge.

Opening the door he was greeted by a nauseous stench. The porthole was closed, the heating was on, and turning on the light he saw the body of a man on the floor. The head lay in a pool of blood

Number 9 dock at Salford today – redeveloped as part of the Salford Quays complex.

and from where he stood there was no doubt the man was dead. The injuries to the upper body were so severe that the face was almost unrecognisable, the only clue to identity being the uniform, which was that of the chief officer.

Locking the cabin behind him, the sailor headed straight for shore and the local police station, and within minutes officers from the Salford Borough Force accompanied him back to the ship. Led by Superintendent Sydney Lawrence, the Assistant Chief Constable, they surveyed the scene in the cabin. The victim was identified as James William Percey, the 48 year old Canadian born chief radio officer.

Lawrence learned that Percey had been paid on the previous Monday and would have been in possession of nearly £80. Was he the victim of a robbery? This seemed likely. The detective went over the cabin with a methodical eye and instead of the £50 or so he would have expected Percey to have left after a few days in port, all he could find was a handful of copper totalling less than five shillings.

39

On a table were three empty beer bottles, two full ones, and two half-empty tumblers. It appeared that Percey had been entertaining in his cabin before the murder. Detective Superintendent Cleminson noticed fingerprints on one of the beer glasses and had them taken to the forensic laboratory to see if there was a matching set of prints on file.

Percey had been a strong man but he did not seem to have put up any resistance, which suggested that he had been friendly with his killer and taken by surprise. A young detective, on his first murder case, carefully picked up a bloodstained bottle and suggested, 'This looks like it might have been the weapon,' but Cleminson reasoned that if a bottle had been used it would certainly have shattered, judging from the extent of the injuries. A search in the adjacent berth found a bloodstained axe concealed beneath a bunk, and this proved to be the murder weapon.

The police surgeon called to examine the body immediately after discovery was also new to a murder investigation, and a combination of the effects of the heat of the cabin and his relative inexperience caused him to state the likely time of death as about a week ago. The Home Office pathologist who later carried out the post-mortem reported that this initial calculation as to the time of death was wrong. 'More likely been dead two days, probably the previous Thursday,' he told the detectives.

As in all murder cases the first steps were to eliminate the obvious suspects: in this case they were Percey's shipmates, if only because they had had the opportunity for murder. Military police rounded the men up and they were interviewed at the docks. Each was able to prove his innocence and in doing so gave a clearer picture of the dead man.

Percey was the archetypal loner, preferring his own company to that of his colleagues. He was a widower, born in Montreal, with no relatives or real friends in England, although he was known to have spent much of his time on previous visits to Salford in the company of a local prostitute called Maureen. He kept himself to himself on ship and was fond of a drink, but although he spent a lot of time in the dockside pubs he didn't have many friends amongst those who gathered there. Yet he seemed to have invited someone into his cabin.

It had been the Monday morning after they docked before Percey finally went ashore, making his way to the Marconi Naval Offices in Liverpool, where he collected his wages, a large sum of back pay,

James William Percey.

and money owed to him by the Board of Trade as compensation for personal goods lost when he was torpedoed on an earlier voyage.

One of the crew told police he had seen Percey drinking with Maureen on the Wednesday, when he had asked the chief for the key to the radio room, so that he could listen to the news broadcast.

'Make sure you lock it, I've a lot of notes in there,' Percey told him as he handed over the key.

'Did you lock it?' the detective asked.

'Yes, I double checked as I left.'

'Did you see the money?'

'I wasn't looking for it,' the sailor replied coldly.

The investigation centred on events that had taken place in the week between the ship docking at Salford and the discovery of the body. Maureen, the prostitute, was able to piece together most of the previous week. Percey had been with her from Tuesday afternoon until lunchtime on Thursday when he told her he needed to return to his ship. They arranged to meet up again later that evening.

'Did he turn up?' asked Cleminson.

'No, he didn't! By the time he set out for his ship he was rolling drunk,' she said. 'I assumed he must have slept through.'

No one had seen the big Canadian after Thursday afternoon, when a dock worker saw him, in the company of another officer, staggering towards the ship at about 3 pm.

'What state was he in?' enquired the detective.

'He appeared to be drunk, and the other officer was holding him up.'

Arriving on board ship with his companion, Percey had called in to see the second mate. He collected his keys and purchased half a dozen bottles of beer, inviting the second mate to join them when he came off duty.

Shortly before 5 pm, the second mate called at the cabin and found it closed. Assuming that the party had finished and the men had gone ashore, he returned to his own cabin. Another officer called at Percey's cabin at five o'clock, and he too found it locked. Cleminson concluded therefore, that the time of death was between 3 pm and 5 pm, which tied in perfectly with the pathologist's report.

The investigation now concentrated on the mystery seaman who had accompanied Percey on board ship. Percey must have met his killer after leaving Maureen earlier that afternoon, perhaps in one of the pubs he passed on his way back to the docks. No one had reported seeing the man leave the ship but descriptions given by those who had seen him enter the dock yards suggested that he was a chief steward in the Mercantile Navy.

Cleminson had a photograph of Percey enlarged and posted outside the docks and the dockside pubs, under the banner: 'Have You Seen This Man?' Several witnesses responded and one in particular gave detectives the best description so far of the steward who boarded the *Shipper* with Percey, adding that the mystery officer was wearing a shabby bridge coat.

Fortunately, no merchant ships had left since the discovery of the body, although most had selected their crews, loaded up, and were ready to sail. Detectives interviewed all the chief stewards on vessels that had been in the dock since before the murder but they were all clear.

A listing of all sailors registered with the pool and awaiting a posting was obtained and on Tuesday morning, 11th April, the two detectives returned to the docks. As they strode across the yard they were met by the cargo supervisor from one of the ships.

'Found that chap who killed Jim Percey yet?' he asked them.

'Why, do you know something?' the detective replied.

'Well, I've thought of something,' he went on. 'I saw Jim drinking before the weekend with a couple of chief stewards. One of them I know, and his ship is still in Salford.'

Detectives visited the chief steward on his boat, where they learned that the man they wanted was named James Galbraith.

James Galbraith was 26 years old and since the break-up of his marriage had been living locally with his mother at Moss Road, Stretford. He had a criminal record, which was one of the reasons why he had been unable to secure a position on one of the ships in the port. He was known to be short of cash – his drawings from the pool were only £3 a week, and he had recently asked for a loan from the pool fund. A check of his records produced a set of prints which matched those on one of the glasses in Percey's cabin. The police now had a prime suspect and set about bringing him in for questioning.

Officers visited his mother who told them he had not been home for several days – since the weekend. She said he had been working at the docks and had given her £2 towards his keep. Fortunately, the old lady still had the notes and the numbers matched those issued to Percey by the Marconi offices. They asked to look around her son's room and took away a number of personal effects, one of which was a shabby bridge coat. That evening, shortly before 11 pm, he was seen approaching the house. No sooner had he entered the front door than he was under arrest.

Back at the station Galbraith was interrogated and denied everything, but being left to stew in a cell for a couple of hours seemed to shake him up, and when re-interviewed later the next morning he admitted meeting Percey as he walked back towards his ship, but still denied murder.

'He was drunk and asked me the way to Number Nine Dock. Being in no hurry I offered to show him the way, but left him to board the ship alone.'

When told that his prints had been found in the cabin, Galbraith changed the last bit of his statement and admitted going there to share a drink.

'Capital Punishment Amendment Act, 1868

(31 & 32 Vict. c. 24, s. 7)

The sentence of the law passed upon *JAMES GALBRAITH* found guilty of murder, will be carried into execution at *9* a.m. to-morrow.

Perry Macdonald Sheriff of *Lancashire.*

C. T. Cepe Governor.

25th July 1944

Manchester Prison.

No. 278.

An execution notice.

'I noticed that when he opened his drawer there was a wad of notes lying in the top corner, nearest the settee. Percey closed the drawer and sat down again. We were talking. Then he went out of the cabin leaving me alone with my beer. While he was out, seeing the money in the drawer there tempted me and I opened the drawer and took a handful of the notes. I could not say whether I took the lot, but I don't think so. I didn't count the money until I was back in the port when I found I had stolen around £36.'

When asked by Lawrence if he had any objection to being held for further questioning, Galbraith replied, 'The only objection I have is that I didn't kill the man, and I know nothing about it.'

Investigations revealed that Galbraith had been spending money in a carefree fashion, which included £8 on a new bridge coat. Much of the dead man's money was used to treat a soldier's wife to a weekend of luxury, while he also paid back an old friend the pound note he had been promising for weeks. Police recovered most of the notes Galbraith spent, all of which were traced to Percey. All told, Galbraith spent over £35 in four days.

The final piece of evidence against the prisoner was supplied by Dr Firth at the Preston forensic laboratory. Traces of blood found on the sleeve of the tattered bridge coat matched the blood group of the dead man, and several witnesses had testified that Galbraith was wearing a similar coat when seen boarding the ship. Also found on clothing in his bedroom at Stretford, were a number of hairs which had come from the victim.

Galbraith's three day trial at Manchester Assizes at the beginning of May was little more than a formality. The defence counsel admitted the theft but claimed that Percey was very much still alive when Galbraith pocketed the notes and fled. Asked to consider the verdict, the jury were clearly unimpressed with Galbraith's version of events and needed only a short time to find him guilty. James Percey, drunk and lonely, had invited a stranger in for a drink and lost his life for that gesture of friendship. Mr Justice Hilberry donned the black cap and the court sat in silence as he pronounced sentence of death. On a warm Wednesday morning, 26th July, 1944, James Galbraith was hanged at Strangeways prison.

7

THE BODY ON THE BEACH

THE MURDER OF JOYCE JACQUES AT MORECAMBE, APRIL 1946

Joyce Jacques, a pretty 22 year old brunette, was determined to enjoy herself despite the austerity of post-war life. She was regularly to be found in one or another of Morecambe's dance halls and ballrooms, enjoying the attentions of young soldiers eager to put the war behind them.

On 5th April, 1946, she met Walter Clayton, married and recently demobbed, while out dancing. Many a marriage had been unsettled since the end of the war, and the two began an intense and passionate affair, spending every night together at her lodgings. Just seven days later, she was dead.

Her body was discovered at 9.45 pm on Friday, 12th April by a young girl returning home from the cinema, lying on the foreshore near the Beach Street bus stop, immediately under the sea wall. It was clear that she had been strangled – a scarf was still tightly knotted around her neck and her tongue protruded, making the body a grotesque sight. There was no sign of sexual interference and her clothing was not dishevelled, which suggested that she had been killed at the spot where she was found.

Superintendent Hogg and Inspector Price from Morecambe CID took charge of the investigation. A wire was sent to the headquarters of the Lancashire Constabulary and Superintendent Floyd and Detective Superintendent Woodmansey from Blackburn and Preston respectively, were informed and travelled at once to the town. Within the hour a wireless car and bloodhounds were at the scene. A generator was set up and police searched for clues under powerful arc lights, while a crowd of curious locals gathered to watch from a distance.

Papers found in Joyce's handbag, recovered from beside her body,

Police officers searching Morecambe beach under the direction of Inspector Price. *(Morecambe Visitor)*

led police to an address at Christie Avenue, Morecambe. It was approaching midnight when detectives called at the house and broke the news of the tragedy. The occupier was Mrs Doris Walker and in tears she told police a little about the victim.

Joyce was a native of Barnsley but had moved to Morecambe in her childhood, when her parents split up, and had been living there with her mother and stepfather when war broke out. In 1941 she had enlisted in the WAAFs and rose to the rank of Flight Sergeant before her discharge. On leaving the force, she had begun training as a nurse but this only lasted a short time and she took a job in a local laundry. Towards the end of the war she had divided her time between her grandparents in Barnsley and her mother in Morecambe, but when her mother died in December 1945 she had moved in with Mrs Walker.

Joyce's reputation as something of a 'good time girl' gave the police their first indication of a possible motive for her murder. From Mrs Walker they learned of her recent intense relationship. Asked who the boyfriend was, she told them he was called 'Pat', and from letters found in Joyce's room, they learned that his real name was Walter Clayton.

Clayton was 22 years old and had recently returned from serving in Burma and the Far East. He was a native of Clitheroe, Lancashire, where he had married his wife soon after war broke out, but when her husband was posted overseas, Mrs Clayton had returned to live with her parents in Morecambe. On his discharge from the army, Clayton came to Morecambe to stay with his wife while they sorted out a place of their own.

When Superintendent Floyd and Detective Constable Williams visited the house in Balmoral Road at 2.30 next morning, Clayton opened the door. They were shown into the lounge where Clayton's wife and mother-in-law stood in their dressing gowns. Clayton faced the detectives, and after looking over his shoulder towards his wife, he said, 'I know what you've come about. I suppose you've found her. Don't say anything here.'

He was taken by police car to the local station, where he spoke freely of his affair with Joyce Jacques. He had spent the first night with her at Christie Avenue, and also the subsequent five nights, returning each morning to his 'home' on Balmoral Road. What his in-laws thought about this arrangement was never made clear. On 10th April the first signs of friction had appeared, Joyce seeming to be on the verge of leaving him. They had quarrelled, but soon made it up.

On the night of the murder they met up and went on a pub crawl, starting in The Battery and visiting five different pubs during the evening before finishing in The Elms. Clayton's statement baldly described what followed. 'On returning to The Elms, Joyce said that she felt a little drunk, so we decided to go for a stroll along the front, where we had a quarrel and I strangled her with my silk scarf. I then left her on the beach and carried on by taxi to The Battery.'

Later Clayton went to the Central Pier to find his wife, who was spending the evening there dancing. Curiously polite, he waited for the dance to finish before asking her to 'go for a stroll, to which she gave permission.' Then followed the painful admittance of his love for Joyce and his dreadful crime. Yet his wife was not about to forsake him, even now. She asked if she could go to the scene of the crime – perhaps doubting if things could actually be as awful as Walter made out – but on his refusing she simply 'asked me to go home with her for the last time.'

Less than six hours after the body had been discovered, Clayton was charged with murder. When searched, police found four rings belonging to the dead girl, all gifts from different soldiers, and presumably what caused Clayton to become jealous and kill her.

On Wednesday, 16th July, Walter Clayton stood trial at Manchester Assizes. Wearing his khaki uniform which sported his service medals and chevrons, he glanced around the court rubbing his nose nervously and as the charge was read out he replied, 'Guilty, my Lord!'

The judge, Mr Justice Stable, leaned forward and asked him a number of questions.

'Clayton, do you fully understand the nature of the charge to which you have pleaded guilty?'

'Yes, my Lord.'

'You appreciate what pleading guilty to this charge – that you took this woman's life with no mitigating circumstances – involves?'

'Yes, my Lord.'

When the Commissioner of the Assizes asked him if he had anything to say why sentence of death should not be passed, Clayton replied in a firm voice, 'No, my Lord.'

The prisoner's eyes were fixed on the floor as the judge donned the black cap and pronounced sentence. The whole proceedings took less than three minutes, and as Clayton was ushered from the dock his wife could be heard sobbing loudly at the back of the court. On a warm summer morning, 7th August, 1946, he was hanged for his crime of passion at Walton prison, Liverpool.

8

'ONE OF MY FUNNY MOODS'

THE MURDER OF NANCY CHADWICK AT RAWTENSTALL, AUGUST 1948

On Sunday morning, 28th August, 1948, hundreds of townsfolk gathered on the riverbank at Rawtenstall. There hadn't been a murder in the town for as long as anyone could remember, and as the news spread like wildfire, curiosity brought out the sightseers as police in wading boots searched the river close to the spot where the body of 68 year old Mrs Nancy Ellen Chadwick had been found a few hours earlier.

Men returning home from a union meeting at the bus station at the end of Bacup Road had discovered the body of the frail old lady in the road. Assuming that she was the victim of a hit and run accident, they had returned to the depot and the police were called. At 4.15 am the police surgeon found that the old lady had been dead for about ten hours, effectively ruling out any chance of her being the victim of a hit and run. An examination of the body had found a number of wounds to the back of the head, caused very probably by a blunt instrument.

Later that morning police officers had interviewed the occupants of the houses on Bacup Road and asked if they had seen or heard anything suspicious on the previous night. There were no reports of anything untoward and at lunch time Chief Superintendent Woodmansey of Lancashire CID made a telephone call to Scotland Yard asking for assistance. As Chief Inspector Stevens and his sergeant travelled up from London on the first available train, the local police began their search for the murder weapon.

Amongst those who congregated on the riverbank was 42 year old Margaret Allen, known locally as Maggie Smith, outside whose house

50

Maggie Allen. *(Lancashire Evening Telegraph)*

51

at 137 Bacup Road the body was discovered. She actually preferred to be called 'Bill' and made no secret of her lesbianism, always wearing men's clothing and sporting a distinctive Eton crop. She appeared keen to help in the search. 'Look, there's a bag in the water,' she shouted to officers wading in the water. Pointing to a spot some yards upstream, she called out again, 'There it is, up yonder.'

A detective followed her directions and pulled out a string shopping bag containing a brown handbag which belonged to the dead woman. Inside were a number of items, mostly personal things, and as there was no sign of her purse, this seemed to confirm the theory that the frail old lady had been battered to death for the contents of her purse.

Despite her scruffy appearance, Mrs Chadwick was reported to be a wealthy woman, an assumption which had probably led to her being attacked and robbed of a large sum of money two years earlier. She had been a widow since 1921 and was thought by many in the town to be a bit eccentric, a trait not helped by her frequent wanderings through the streets begging and then counting her money in the park. It was often wondered why she should resort to begging when it was common knowledge that a former employer, a wealthy stonemason, had left her a number of houses in his will and she was known to collect the rent on these properties fortnightly. Since the end of the war she had been working as a housekeeper for an elderly man who lived at Hardmin Avenue on the Hill Carr Estate.

One other aspect of her life was her reputation as a fortune teller. She was often called upon to predict people's destiny, which she did with both playing cards and tea leaves. Did she predict her own fate?

Believing that they were searching for a callous thief and anxious to interview anyone who had seen Mrs Chadwick on the last day of her life, officers issued a description of the clothes she was last seen wearing. They were a grey, single-breasted coat with large buttons on the front, a brown woollen dress, brown stockings, pale green ankle socks and black shoes. This description was flashed on screens in many cinemas in and around East Lancashire but met with little success.

As no one reported seeing anyone suspicious in the area, Chief Inspector Stevens thought that the killer was probably a local man and officers raided the houses of a number of likely suspects and took away items of clothing for forensic tests.

Margaret Allen had made one statement to police after the murder,

Maggie Allen's house. The building is still standing although a large part of the front of the building has been demolished. *(Lancashire Evening Telegraph)*

as had her neighbours, but Chief Inspector Stevens decided to pay her another visit on Wednesday morning. 'Bill' was a sad and lonely woman. A bus conductoress during the war, the death of her mother in 1943 seemed to have broken her spirit and she had not worked for three years. Self-neglect had led to illness and at one point she needed medical treatment for attacks of dizziness.

Whatever suspicions her original statement had aroused in Stevens were amply rewarded when he stepped inside the tiny two-room sandstone terrace house. He immediately noticed what appeared to be bloodstains on the wall behind the front door, and a search upstairs produced a bag containing several stained cloths.

He asked Maggie to explain them, and looking him in the eye she replied, 'Come on, I'll tell you all about it. But not here.' Picking up her raincoat she beckoned the officers out of the door, but not before pointing to the cellar and admitting, 'That is where I put her.'

At Rawtenstall police station, she was placed in an interview room and told Stevens as he sat facing her, 'I didn't do it for money. I was in one of my funny moods.' After receiving a caution, she then dictated a lengthy statement in which she coldly described how she had committed the murder.

> 'I was coming out of the house on Saturday morning, about 9.20 am, and Mrs Chadwick came around the corner. She asked me if this was where I lived and could she come in? I told her I was going out. I was in a nervy mood and she just seemed to get on my nerves even though she had not said anything. I told her to go and that she could see me some time else, but she seemed to insist on coming in. I happened to look around and saw a hammer in the kitchen. At this time we were talking just inside the kitchen with the front door shut. On the spur of the moment I hit her with the hammer. She gave a shout which seemed to start me off more. I hit her a few times but I don't know how many. I then pulled the body into my coal house.'

After the murder she had called on a friend and gone shopping before spending the afternoon with one of her sisters at Bacup, returning to Rawtenstall in the early evening where she spent the rest of the night in The Ashworth Arms.

Thursday, 2nd September, was Margaret's 43rd birthday and the day on which she was charged with murder and committed for trial at Manchester Assizes.

The defence at her trial in December was led by William Gorman KC, later to become Mr Justice Gorman. He described to the court Margaret's frustration at being born a woman, and her failed suicide attempts, but his efforts to prove her insanity were in vain. The prosecution's case that she had murdered for gain was supported by her calm and lucid confession to the police, and the jury took just 15 minutes to find Margaret Allen guilty of murder.

There was no recommendation for mercy. Margaret Allen was one of only a handful of convicted murderers who declined to appeal against the sentence, choosing to accept her fate 'like a man'.

As she waited in the condemned cell she had one friend working on her behalf – 34 year old Annie Cook, who had been friendly with Margaret since the end of the war, and attempted to collect a petition for reprieve in Rawtenstall, but out of a population of 26,000 only 126 signed.

On 12th January, 1949, Margaret Allen was hanged at Strangeways, the first woman to be executed since 1936. Denied her usual male clothing, 'Bill' was forced to meet her fate wearing a regulation striped prison frock.

9

HANGMAN'S LAMENT

THE MURDER OF ELIZA WOOD AT ASHTON-UNDER-LYNE, AUGUST 1950

The county of Lancashire provided the country with more than its share of hangmen throughout the late 19th and 20th centuries, the most famous being Albert Pierrepoint, who ran a public house on the outskirts of Manchester. One of the strangest cases at which he officiated involved a man he not only knew well, but who had often joined him in singing a bar-room duet.

James Henry Corbitt, a 37 year old engineer, had a clear tenor voice and, dressed in a cheap blue suit and multi-coloured bow tie, was a popular if somewhat mysterious figure in pubs and clubs around Ashton-under-Lyne. On the evening of Saturday, 19th August, 1950, he was drinking at the curiously named Help the Poor Struggler pub on the Oldham Road. Here he was sure of a friendly greeting from the landlord who, when trade was slow, would join him in a song. Tonight they shared a quick chorus and later, as he and his woman companion left the landlord bid them goodnight with the friendly remark, 'Night, Tish.' Smiling at the landlord, the singer replied, 'Goodnight, Tosh.'

Shortly before midnight the couple returned to their hotel, the Prince of Wales on Stamford Street. The woman was very much the worse for drink, having to be half-carried up the stairs, and twice during the night the landlord had to bang on the door and warn them to keep the noise down.

Early next morning Corbitt came down the stairs and announced that he was going to take a walk. 'There's no need to take up a cup of tea, my wife doesn't want one,' he told Margaret Bailey, the cleaner, before slipping out of the front door. Turning up his collar against the wind, he quickly glanced around before disappearing down the street. Something about his furtive manner left the cleaner

Help the Poor Struggler public house.

with an uneasy feeling and after setting the breakfast table, she poured a cup of tea and set off for room seven.

Receiving no reply to her knocking, Mrs Bailey took out a pass key and entered the darkened room. Walking across to the heavy drapes she flung them back and recoiled in horror at the sight that greeted her. Lying on one of the twin beds was the naked body of a middle-aged woman. Blazoned across her forehead, printed in one inch tall letters of blue ink, was the word WHORE.

At 8.40 am the landlord Mr Egan picked up the telephone and summoned the police. Within the hour Detective Chief Superintendent Lindsay of Lancashire CID arrived, accompanied by Dr Grace, the Home Office pathologist, who certified that the woman was dead. The doctor gave the cause of death as manual strangulation, despite a series of grooves in the neck probably made by a broken bead necklace found on the bedroom floor. In the woman's handbag they found papers that revealed her identity to be 36 year old Mrs Eliza Wood.

On Monday, 6th November, 1950, James Corbitt stood trial at Liverpool Assizes, Mr Justice Lynskey presiding. Corbitt entered the dock and smiled at his estranged wife in the public gallery, and in a firm voice he replied 'Not guilty' to the charge.

In fact, Corbitt had admitted to police that he had killed Eliza, but accidentally, and the court case was to hinge on whether Corbitt was sane at the time of the attack.

Edward Wooll KC, for the prosecution, told the jury to be prepared to hear the tale of a squalid, morbid, repugnant tragedy. The accused was a married man living apart from his wife, the victim was a married woman with two young children living apart from her husband. Mrs Eliza Wood had lived in Oldham, a few streets away from her mother's house where Corbitt had been a lodger since the autumn of 1949, and where Eliza was a frequent visitor to the house. Gradually the couple began a relationship and in July Corbitt left these lodgings and took a room in Ashton, where he was staying up until the time of his arrest.

Corbitt had left a remarkable chronicle of their relationship in the form of a diary, which the prosecution was to use to show how he had planned the murder early in the year, the entries continuing until the day before the murder. Opening the diary, Wooll read out a selection of entries starting with:

February 21st: 'Liza told me after being intimate with her. I nearly strangled her.'

March 11th: 'Date with Liza 8.30 pm. Waited till 10 pm. Will not wait again. My intentions are to win her affections completely and when she cannot do without me I will play my final card.'

The prosecution alleged that the final card was played on 19th August. Wooll then selected a number of other entries:

July 13th: 'Took Liza out for drinks ... a miracle saved her.'

July 23rd: 'Took Liza out tonight. Got her drunk ... Could have finished her but was just toying with her.'

August 12th: 'She must have been born under a lucky star ... I would have finished her on Saturday night.'

When it was the turn of the defence to present their case they too focused on the diary, which they claimed showed the prisoner's mental state. Mr Rosen KC pointed to the entry for 19th March, which mentioned:

'. . . headaches all day. I am insane and must proceed cautiously.'
Another entry on 30th March referred to:

'. . . mental strain . . . mind is a blank . . . impossible to sleep today.'

Rosen, in a 20 minute address to the jury, said that Corbitt was a decent, respectable man up until the break up of his marriage, when

Strangeways prison today – where James Corbitt paid for his crime.

Albert Pierrepoint. Such was Mr Pierrepoint's notoriety that he had his own publicity photograph produced to sign and give away over the bar of his pub.

he took to drinking and began an affair with a married woman. The facts of the case were clear, but he asked the jury to find the accused guilty but insane, citing the entries in the diary and statements made by Corbitt when arrested. No medical witnesses were called.

Mr Justice Lynskey directed the jury that in order to find the prisoner guilty but insane they must satisfy themselves on three counts: that the accused was suffering from a disease of the mind; that the disease produced a defect in his reasoning; and lastly that this defect was of such a character that he was unable to appreciate the nature of his act, or if he did appreciate it, that he was unable to appreciate that it was wrong.

The judge's summing up lasted almost 45 minutes. Was James

Corbitt insane? The jury evidently did not think so. They needed just 20 minutes to find Corbitt guilty of premeditated murder and he was sentenced to death. An appeal was lodged on his behalf but to no avail and Corbitt was taken to the condemned cell at Strangeways to await the hangman.

On Monday afternoon, 27th November, public hangman Albert Pierrepoint and his assistant Harry Allen settled into their quarters and prepared to rig up the scaffold for the following morning. Pierrepoint was handed the condemned man's details and asked about the prisoner. The warder said that Corbitt was in good spirits considering the circumstances, but kept telling them that he was a friend of the hangman and seemed more worried that Pierrepoint would not remember him than about his impending doom. 'I hope Albert will let on he knows me, it will make it easier for me,' he kept repeating.

Next morning on the stroke of nine, the hangmen entered the cell. Corbitt looked up and muttered weakly, 'Hello, Tosh.' Pierrepoint smiled back and replied, 'Hello, Tish.' Helping him to his feet, Pierrepoint whispered, 'Come on, old chap,' and Corbitt strolled to the gallows as if a weight had been lifted from his shoulders.

A couple of hours later the hangmen left the prison. As Pierrepoint stood behind his bar that afternoon he may have reflected that Corbitt was probably the only murderer ever to sing a duet with his executioner.

10

MURDER ON THE MOORS

THE MURDER OF RADOMIR DJOROVIC AT ROSSENDALE, OCTOBER 1950

At first light on the morning of 9th October, 1950, a gang of railwaymen making repairs on the Accrington – Bury line across the Rossendale Valley discovered the body of 26 year old Radomir Djorovic in an old trackside hut, his head lying in a pool of blood. The murder hunt which followed awoke wartime memories of old griefs and hatreds in far-off Yugoslavia, where both Djorovic and his murderer had been born and lived until the end of the Second World War, when they began a new life in the mill town of Blackburn.

The officer in charge of the investigation was Detective Chief Superintendent Lindsay, the head of Lancashire CID, assisted by Chief Superintendent Platt. Their first task was identifying the body. As officers combed the surrounding area in search of clues, police learned that a Yugoslav man had failed to arrive the previous day for Sunday lunch at the small hamlet of Edenfield, and early next morning his girlfriend, Ankiea Mileusnic, identified the body.

The investigation soon turned up a prime suspect. Detectives visited a lodging house on Caton Street in the Mill Hill area of Blackburn and found that 29 year old Nenad Kovacevic, a friend of the dead man, had fled. They learned that he had gone to Blackpool to catch a coach to London, as the Blackburn to London coach only ran once a week and was fully booked. Investigations in Blackpool found that on Tuesday morning he had left on the London bound bus.

Lindsay radioed ahead and set up a road block. The coach was scheduled to call at Newcastle-under-Lyme, Staffordshire, and when they missed the connection by a matter of minutes, officers from Staffordshire CID stopped the bus at Cannock bus station.

Kovacevic was arrested on suspicion of murder and taken into custody. He denied any part in the murder and said he had spent the afternoon with his Hungarian girlfriend, Liza Siegbert. He was shown a number of items taken from his lodgings which belonged to the murdered man, and at first made no comment, but then he broke down and said he was sorry that he had killed his friend. Lindsay, who had travelled to Cannock by fast car, formally charged him with the wilful murder of his fellow countryman.

Nenad Kovacevic stood trial at Manchester Assizes on 7th December, 1950, before Mr Justice Jones. He pleaded not guilty.

The prosecution case was that the murder was premeditated, the motive being that Kovacevic was short of money. Items found in his room proved that he had stolen from the victim and his landlady testified that he had been unable to pay his rent on the Saturday before the murder, but at 5 pm on Sunday, with Djorovic lying dead in the cabin, Kovacevic paid off some of the arrears. Later that Sunday night, he took Liza and her friend, Bella Lang, out and spent money in a lavish style, and after escorting both girls home in a taxi he gave Bella a cigarette case identified as belonging to Djorovic. Kovacevic had then fled to London in the hope of avoiding arrest.

Mr Kenneth Burke, who led for the defence, put forward a plea of guilty of manslaughter, brought on by intense provocation. Kovacevic's account of the events of that day was very different to that of the police, and was to earn him considerable support.

On 8th October, as rain clouds hovered ominously in the black sky over the bleak West Pennine Moors, the two men had set out from their Blackburn homes for Edenfield, the small hamlet several miles away where two sisters, also Yugoslavs, had promised to cook Sunday lunch.

The men set off across the moors and decided to speed up the journey time by taking a short-cut down the railway line. As they approached Ewood Bridge, in the heart of the Rossendale Valley, the heavens opened up, and spying a small trackside hut in the distance they headed for shelter.

As they sheltered from the downpour, Kovacevic's thoughts went back to 1943, seven years to the day, when his family had been cruelly massacred by the advancing German army. He had been away from home at the time, fighting in the hills with the resistance, and only learned of their fate weeks later. As he remembered, tears filled his eyes and he began to sob. Djorovic saw the sadness in his friend's face and asked what was up. When told, Djorovic scoffed and told him that he had sided with the Germans, admitting he had

Radomir Djorovic. *(Lancashire Evening Telegraph)*

sympathised with Hitler and had helped the Germans to sniff out a number of resistance workers.

Kovacevic seethed in anger. Djorovic carried on taunting his friend, and began to slap him about the head. Finally Kovacevic lost control. Glancing around the hut, he spotted a workman's axe lying beside the door and in a rage he picked it up and struck his

64

compatriot around the head several times. Djorovic slumped to the floor; the blows had fractured his skull, killing him instantly.

The prisoner, continued Mr Burke, had made no preparation for the crime, which was in no way planned, and although he admitted that it bore certain hallmarks of a premeditated attack, the truth was that Kovacevic had simply lost control after being driven into a frenzy by taunts and blows. The bruises on the prisoner's face when arrested backed this up.

Burke also claimed that although Kovacevic had taken a number of items from the dead man, he didn't do this deliberately, as the items had been in the victim's raincoat pocket, and he had only taken the coat to avoid getting a soaking from the heavy rain. He added that although Kovacevic had been unable to pay his rent on Saturday, this was not a motive for murder, it was merely coincidental.

Kovacevic had planned to report the murder on Sunday night, but decided to visit a friend in London to ask for advice before going to the police. The prisoner was not attempting to escape, merely seeking legal advice before surrender. Mr Burke concluded by asking for sympathy, bearing in mind that his family had been massacred during the war.

The jury took 85 minutes to return a verdict of guilty of murder and when asked if he had anything to say before sentence was passed, Kovacevic replied in English, 'I can't say anything, I killed him.' He was then sentenced to death through an interpreter. There was a short delay in the translation when the interpreter couldn't find the equivalent word for 'thence' in the passage: '... thence to a place of execution ...'

There was an immediate appeal, based on the judge's summing up, which his council claimed was biased in favour of the prosecution, but it was quickly rejected by Lord Chief Justice Goddard. Strenuous efforts were made for a reprieve and King Peter, the former ruler of Yugoslavia, made a personal plea for clemency, but it was all to no avail.

On the night before his execution Kovacevic asked if he could see his girlfriend for the last time and a taxi was sent to her home in Accrington which took her to Strangeways prison for a farewell meeting.

At 8 am on 26th January, 1951, Nenad Kovacevic was hanged at Manchester. The Yugoslav had had to fight all his life; and as Pierrepoint tried to pinion his arms, he kicked out and had to be dragged to the drop fighting all the way.

11

REVENGE AT THE WAKES

THE MURDER OF MONA MATHER AT TYLDESLEY, APRIL 1951

Mona Mather could scarcely have made a worse choice for a boyfriend when she started courting Jack Wright, a Tyldesley coal miner, during the summer of 1950. Gregarious and flighty, she flirted outrageously with anyone whenever she and Jack went out as a couple. Unknown to Mona she was playing with fire and asking to get burned.

On a cold, rainy autumn night later that year, while the couple were out strolling in a rainswept park, 28 year old Mona spotted an old boyfriend and in an instant they began chatting away, oblivious to Jack who stood quietly at her side, unafforded the shelter of the umbrella which her recently re-acquainted friend was now sharing.

Eventually Jack turned to Mona and complained, 'Don't you think it's time we were getting back?' Without so much as a backward glance she replied, 'Oh, you can go if you want, I'll catch up with you again.' She wasn't to know it, but Mona had just had a very lucky escape.

Six months after the episode in the rain, fate finally caught up with Mona Mather. The annual Easter fair – 'the wakes' – was being held on Shakerley Common, Tyldesley, a small town west of Manchester.

Early on Saturday evening, 7th April, 1951, Jack Wright met up with a few of his workmates and went out drinking, visiting several local pubs before finishing up at The George and Dragon at just before 10 pm. Jack had hardly settled down with a drink when he felt a tap on the shoulder and spun round to find himself face to face with the girl he had last seen laughing at him as he walked out of her life several months before.

Mona had left her home at Wharton Fold, Little Hulton, earlier that evening and was out with her brother Joe and his wife, having a few

```
bouts,  (28),  1,  Wharton  Fol
 pneu-  Hulton.  He  was  rem:
orning  custody  until  April  18
g him  aid being granted.
 news-    Wright,  a  fair  hair(
0-40 to  complexioned  man  of
les she                    heigh
r hus-                     an  c
 kind,                     s h i 1
le had                     pullo
is life,                   n a v
 being                     suit.
 being                     Supt
                           M e r
e and                      lated
tificial                   cums
al of a                    the
l  life                    of  t
                           and
andre-                     m  e
```

Mona Mather. *(Bolton Evening News)*

drinks before going on to the wakes. They had done the round of pubs in Tyldesley but Mona had failed to find a date to accompany her to the fair and, spotting Jack, she homed in at once.

Both had a fair bit to drink and when she asked Jack if he wanted to sleep with her tonight he forgot about the events of the past and nodded his head in agreement. Finishing their drinks, Jack and Mona set out for the fair together, leaving The George and Dragon at 10.25 pm, bidding goodnight to her brother and his wife who left them outside and made their own way to the fair.

They spent an hour or so on the various amusements and it was during one of the rides, as Jack caught sight of her laughing wildly, that he decided that tonight he would get his revenge.

With midnight fast approaching, he asked her if she would like him to walk her home. Mona slipped her arm through his, smiled, and said 'Yes, please'. As they left the fair they were spotted by one of Jack's workmates, Matthew Weir, who shouted across at him, 'Well, Jackie, I didn't know you were courting!' Jack looked across and replied, 'No. This is one I have picked up!'

They walked for the best part of a half hour; along the common, past a brickworks and over a railway footbridge before turning onto a path that led alongside the Wharton Hall Colliery pumping station situated close to the Tyldesley and Little Hulton border. They stopped against a fence and began to kiss. Mona closed her eyes as his powerful hands held her closely. Suddenly he reached up to her neck and squeezed it tightly.

Seconds later, as she slumped almost lifeless against him, he heard voices coming down the nearby footpath. Silently he stood in the shadows as a young couple strolled by almost within touching distance.

Satisfying himself that the coast was clear, he carried her sagging body into the field beside the colliery and set about the task, taking his time, almost relishing the thrill of the kill. Kneeling over her, Jack pulled off the white silk scarf Mona had had draped over her coat and knotted it tightly around her neck.

Contemporary news photograph of the murder scene. *(Bolton Evening News)*

Certain that she was now dead, he took off her coat and threw it over the lifeless body, taking a last look round before disappearing into the night. He then went home and ate a large supper before retiring to bed.

At six the next morning, 43 year old Fred Broad finished his shift at Wharton colliery and headed home across the field. Crossing the path that dissected the waste ground adjacent to the pit, Fred noticed a strange bundle on the ground and curiosity caused him to take a closer look. Moments later he found himself staring down at the body of a woman; her grotesquely distorted features left him in no doubt she was dead, so he rushed off to inform the police of his gruesome discovery.

Within the hour the place was crawling with police. Chief Superintendent Mercer, the head of Leigh police, was the first to arrive, later to be joined by Detective Superintendent Lindsay, Chief Inspector McCartney, Chief Inspector Campbell and both the Assistant and Chief Constables of Lancashire CID. The body had been found lying three yards inside the Little Hulton border. The little money still in her purse suggested that robbery was not the motive for the attack. They concluded their initial report with the thought that she had made her way to the scene of the crime willingly; from the state of her clothing it appeared she had had sex, but whether this was with her consent they could not be certain.

Inside the handbag they found a number of articles and papers that revealed her identity, and later her horrified relatives were able to tell police that Mona had left The George and Dragon on the previous night with a man she had been seeing last summer, and that they were last seen heading towards the fairground.

Pathologist Dr Carragher of Warrington carried out a post-mortem later that morning and confirmed that Mona had died as a result of strangulation and that the thyroid bone in her neck had been fractured. Alan Thompson of the forensic lab at Preston, reported that all Mona's underclothing had been torn.

By noon police had learned that the man Mona had left the fair with was Jack Wright, a 30 year old coal miner living with his mother and stepfather at 3 John Street, Tyldesley. Officers called at his house and found that he had left earlier that morning, presumably going to one of a number of social clubs where he usually played snooker and enjoyed a Sunday lunchtime pint.

News of police inquiries into Jack Wright's whereabouts quickly spread, and when he called into the Tyldesley Liberal Club he was greeted with, 'Eh, Jack, police have been asking about thee.' He made no comment but quickly finished his drink and headed for another club at nearby Astley.

At closing time he took a train into Manchester. He knew that it was only a matter of time before the police caught up with him, but until they did he reasoned that he might as well make the most of his freedom. He wandered aimlessly around Manchester town centre for a while before opting to see a film at the cinema.

It was getting late and although he knew he was certain to be captured if he returned to Tyldesley, Jack called at London Road railway station in Manchester to catch the last train home. Finding that he still had a short time to wait he went into the snack bar and as he settled down with a cup of tea he was spotted by Detective Constable Hart of British Railways Transport Police, who radioed for assistance. At 12.20 am, Wright was arrested by Detective Inspector Roberts and Detective Constables Holmes and Graham.

At 1.00 am, as he was taken by car to a nearby police station, Wright told the arresting officers that he had been with two women that night and that he left Mona at the fairground with two men. He didn't know their names but he did know that they were from Little Hulton and felt sure that she would have walked home with one of them. Wright was then told that he was being taken back to Tyldesley for questioning in connection with the murder of Mona Mather and replied quietly, 'I don't know what happened.'

Later, Wright turned to an officer and asked him, 'Am I supposed to have done this murder?' The officer made no comment. On arrival at Tyldesley he was again questioned and then charged with the murder, to which he replied, 'That's correct.'

Jack Wright stood trial at Liverpool Assizes before Mr Justice Oliver on 12th June, 1951. Mr J. Robertson Crichton KC, his defence counsel, told the jury that he would ask for a verdict of guilty but insane. They claimed that Wright had admitted to them that he had set out that night to kill a woman and it was sheer coincidence that Mona Mather happened to appear on the scene. They also stated that during the last few years, Wright had made three separate assaults on women, but, as each of the victims had been known to him, they had decided not to press charges. Although Wright knew what he had done was wrong, he didn't seem aware of the consequences.

Mr H. Nelson KC, for the prosecution, countered this simply by stating that there was no evidence to support the claim of insanity and that Wright had murdered Mona Mather as a result of her rejecting him the previous year. Neither Dr Cormack, the medical officer at Strangeways gaol, nor another doctor called to examine him, could find any trace of madness and the prosecution therefore asked the court to find him guilty of wilful, premeditated murder. The jury took just under three hours to return a guilty verdict and Wright was sentenced to death.

On 3rd July, 1951, Jack Wright was hanged at Strangeways for a crime he had waited six months to commit.

12

A WORTHLESS ALIBI

**THE MURDER OF BEATRICE RIMMER AT LIVERPOOL,
AUGUST 1951**

Even hardened detectives were sickened by the death of 52 year old widow Beatrice Rimmer in her little terraced house in the Wavertree area of Liverpool.

She was last seen alive shortly after ten o'clock on Sunday 19th August, 1951, when a neighbour saw her, returning from a visit to her son Thomas's house, put the key into the latch of 7 Cranborne Road and enter the darkened hall. Next day, the milk bottles stayed on the doorstep and there were no comings or goings at the house until her son visited in the early evening. Walking towards the front door the former police officer immediately sensed something was amiss. Pushing the morning paper through the letterbox, he bent down, peered inside and had his worst fears confirmed.

Lying in a pool of blood on the hall floor was the battered body of his mother, still wearing her top coat, and clutching the small bunch of flowers he had given her.

Detectives hurried to the scene and Superintendent Taylor of Liverpool CID took charge. The attack had all the hallmarks of a housebreaking – the intruder having entered through a back kitchen window. Since the death of her husband some years earlier the widow had become something of a recluse who, according to local gossip, was sitting on a tidy sum. More than once in the recent past, the house had been the subject of an attempted break-in. It appeared that on this occasion, having failed to find the money, they had waited for Mrs Rimmer, intending to force her to hand it over.

A Home Office pathologist, Dr George Manning, carried out the post-mortem and told detectives they were probably looking for two men, as she had been attacked with two different weapons. One, sporting a sharp edge, had lacerated her face, whilst the other, a

Number 7, Cranborne Road, Wavertree.

blunt weapon – possibly an electric torch – had fractured her skull.

The frail old lady had been subjected to 15 blows to the head, although none would have proved fatal if treated in time. This supported the theory that the injuries were more likely to have been caused by someone trying to extract information, than the work of a homicidal maniac. The detectives were sickened to hear that she had taken a long time to die, her weak cries for help going unheard, slipping in and out of consciousness as her life ebbed away.

A search of the house failed to identify any missing property and there were no fingerprints other than those with legitimate reason to be there.

Police thought they had those responsible a few days later when two young, known house-breakers were picked up. There had been a spate of house break-ins in the area and it was not unreasonable to assume they were the work of the same gang. One of the youths had blood on his clothing but forensic checks found it not to be group A, that of the dead woman, and, unable to connect them to the crime, they were released.

Days turned into weeks as detectives combed the numerous late night cafes, billiard halls, pubs and lodging houses in the busy port but there were to be no leads, other than the sighting of two youths who had alighted from a bus, close to Cranborne Road, earlier on the evening of the murder.

It was almost a month later when word reached Chief Superintendent Balmer, who had cut short his holiday to take over the investigation, that a 19 year old army deserter held at Walton gaol knew the identity of the killers. When interviewed he refused to talk, declaring, 'I'm no squealer.' Skilful persuasion loosened his tongue.

George McClaughlin claimed that a week before the murder he had spoken with a man in an all-night city centre cafe. The man told him he had travelled from Manchester planning to rob a house at Wavertree, and he agreed to join him. At a further meeting the man introduced McClaughlin to another man who was also to take part in the raid. On Friday, 17th August however, two days before the murder, McClaughlin was picked up as a deserter and they carried out the job without him.

The idea for the robbery was simple. A waitress called June Bury was to call at the house and distract the occupant. The men would scale the back wall, enter through the kitchen, grab what they could find and bundle their way out past the startled woman and make off down the street.

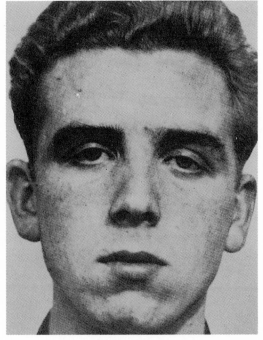

Alfred Burns.

Police interviewed June Bury and she told them the names of the wanted men – 21 year old Alfred Burns of Medlock Street, Manchester, and 22 year old Edward Francis Devlin of Leinster Street, Hulme, Manchester. Despite their relative youth both were seasoned housebreakers boasting a string of convictions across the county.

Balmer knew that he could not order an immediate arrest purely on McClaughlin's testimony, so he assigned scores of detectives to the investigation with the order to question the friends and acquaintances of Burns and Devlin. From June Bury they learned of 17 year old 'Chinese Marie' Milne, Burns's sometime girlfriend, who provided them with a vital breakthrough after reassurance from Balmer that she would not be charged with anything to do with the murder.

Marie frequented various all night cafes, mixing with low-lifes and petty criminals and Balmer's first impression was that she reminded him of a 'moll' from American gangster films. She claimed that Burns had told her he and Devlin planned to do a job in Liverpool and she was asked to come along and act as the lookout. She initially accepted and travelled with them, but was later told she would not be needed and they arranged to meet later.

She told Balmer that when they eventually met up, both men were in a highly agitated state, and Devlin was worried that they might have killed the old lady.

'Don't worry, we'll be well away before long,' Burns had reassured him.

A man interviewed in Liverpool admitted that he had been asked to join them on the robbery on the Friday afternoon, after they had learned of the arrest of McClaughlin. He agreed, but later changed his mind.

Balmer decided to bring the two men in for questioning. On 10th October, Devlin was arrested in a Manchester cafe. He went on the defensive immediately and denied being in Liverpool on the night in question, claiming that he had not even heard of the murder until now. He then said he could not have carried out the murder as he was 'screwing a gaff' in Manchester at the time.

He claimed that he and Burns had been robbing a warehouse in Manchester which had netted them over a hundred raincoats, various other clothes and rolls of material. They finished the job at four o'clock Monday morning, and spent the next few hours trying to steal a vehicle to transport their haul.

Burns was arrested on the following afternoon. He had been taken into custody on the previous day – re-captured as a Borstal absconder – and like Devlin taken to Liverpool for questioning. He also denied the murder but did not offer any alibi except to say that he had been with Devlin throughout August.

They were put up for identification and although the man who had dropped out of the robbery failed to identify them, George McClaughlin pointed them out.

Their clothing was sent for forensic analysis but this proved inconclusive. There were bloodstains on Devlin's suit, which he claimed were the result of a nosebleed sustained in a fight. Tests proved that it matched his own as well as that of the dead woman. Unable to find the murder weapons or any fingerprints that linked either man to the house, Balmer was faced with charging them on the testimony of several undesirables, two of whom had been or still were in prison. It was down to persuading the jury to believe these witnesses, but the experienced officer was certain he had his men.

Edward Francis Devlin.

Burns and Devlin stood trial before Mr Justice Finnimore at Liverpool Assizes on 19th February, 1952. Miss Rose Heilbron QC defended Devlin, while Burns' case was handled by Sir Noel Goldie QC. The prosecution was led by Mr Basil Neild QC. The defence case was simple: no one had seen the accused enter the house or commit murder, the prosecution was relying purely on circumstantial evidence which they planned to refute.

The two accused seemed totally unaffected by the seriousness of the occasion, sniggering at each other and scowling at onlookers up in the public gallery. The trial progressed slowly until the seventh day when Burns' counsel challenged a young detective in the dock.

'Am I right in saying that on the night of the alleged murder a burglary was committed at Sun Blinds Ltd, on Great Jackson Street, Manchester?'

Neild rose to object.

'M'lord, what has this to do with the case?' he protested, but was brushed aside by Mr Goldie who said he didn't want to take his learned friend by surprise later. Goldie said he planned to prove that Burns could not have been in Liverpool on the night in question because he was involved in the aforementioned break-in.

Now 21 year old Alan Campbell was called to the stand. He had been convicted of the offence in Manchester and claimed under oath that he had been accompanied on the job by the two accused.

Burns and Devlin both gave evidence but were unconvincing with their account of the Manchester robbery, with Mr Neild claiming the only information they could offer was that which they could have learned by reading any newspaper reporting the crime. The defence, however, claimed that the Manchester alibi was proven and, as other witnesses had sworn to seeing both men in Manchester on Sunday night, it was unsafe for the jury to convict on the prosecution's evidence.

Challenging the defence, Mr Neild told the court that Campbell had in fact been convicted for a crime committed on *Saturday*, 18th August, 24 hours before the Liverpool murder, thus rendering the alibi little more than worthless.

On the tenth and last day of the trial, the courtroom was packed to capacity. Crowds gathered at first light and hundreds more, unable to gain entry, waited outside for the verdict to be announced.

Speaking for over four hours, Mr Justice Finnimore ended by directing the jury that it was down to which set of witnesses they chose to believe. They needed just 75 minutes to find both Burns and Devlin guilty of murder.

Burns' counsel immediately announced plans for an appeal and asked Lord Chief Justice Goddard and the other appeal judges to allow the unprecedented step of calling new evidence.

A statement, they said, had been made by 15 year old Elizabeth Rooke, a friend of June Bury's, whose testimony had helped convict the men. Bury had told her she had lied about being with Devlin on the night of the murder because she was covering for the real killer, a soldier named 'Auzzey' who was the father of her child. Devlin's sister also made a statement claiming that June Bury had named the killer as a man called McNeill and that he had rewarded June for not altering her statement. On this information, Mr Goldie said, it was unsafe to allow the conviction to stand.

The prosecution claimed that the soldier was one Edward Duffy,

Telephone No. Aintree 2228.

*All communications should be addressed
to " The Governor " (not to any official by
name), and the following number quoted*

....

Your ref. ....

H. M. PRISON,

Liverpool.

2nd April, 1952.

Sydney Dernley, Esq.,

Dear Sir,
No 5736 - E.F. Devlin.

Will you please note that the execution
of the above-named has now been fixed for 9.0 a.m.
on Friday the 18th April, at this Prison.

You will be expected to report at this
establishment not later than 4.0 p.m. on Thursday,
17th April, and a railway warrant is enclosed
for your use. Please acknowledge receipt of this
letter.

Yours faithfully,

C. Mewe

Deputy Governor, i/c.

Letter informing the hangman of the revised date for Devlin's 'appointment'.

but he would not have been able to have committed the murder as he was safely behind bars at Walton gaol during August 1951. June Bury was also questioned again, and under oath she denied both statements.

Dismissing the appeal, the Lord Chief Justice said it was not the duty of the appeal court to hear new evidence, as this must be submitted to those whose duty it was to advise the crown, namely Sir David Maxwell Fyfe, the Home Secretary.

Maxwell Fyfe made legal history when he agreed to launch an inquiry into the investigation, and the date set for the execution, 18th April, was put back a week to allow the report to be compiled. On 21st April the report was published. It claimed that there were no reasonable grounds to suggest that a miscarriage of justice had taken place and the law must take its course. The families of the prisoners petitioned the newly ascended Queen Elizabeth to show mercy but the plea went unheeded.

On Friday, 25th April, 1952, Burns and Devlin were hanged at Walton gaol. A large crowd, including many relatives, protested their innocence and the injustice of the sentences, but two days later a Sunday newspaper alleged that one of them had confessed shortly before execution, and that both were guilty of the horrific murder of Beatrice Rimmer.

13

KILLER OF YOUNG BOYS

THE MURDER OF NORMAN YATES AT WIGAN, APRIL 1955

In August 1954, eleven year old Billy Harmer was knifed to death at Wigan. Intensive police enquiries failed to come up with a suspect for the murder. Then, less than a year later, there was another apparently motiveless, senseless attack on a young boy.

It was Easter Monday, 11th April, 1955 and in houses throughout the country people listened to their radios enthralled as American lawyer Perry Mason successfully defended another client. In the Lower Ince district of Wigan, Jimmy Jones and his friend Walter Wiggins were both enjoying the programme when a piercing scream interrupted their listening.

Darting from his chair, Jones feared that the scream had come from his daughter Doris's bedroom. He dashed upstairs and seeing that Doris was sleeping, he went outside. Opening his front door onto Cross Street, Jones saw that other neighbours had also been alerted by the sound, and lifting the light from Wiggins's bicycle, Jones shouted to his friend, 'Walter, come quickly!', and together they rushed down the street.

As they approached a piece of waste land some 20 yards away, Jones's first thought was that a girl was being assaulted, so high pitched was the scream, but reaching the patch of land he saw a young boy lying whimpering on the ground.

By the light of the bicycle lamp, Jones could see the boy was bleeding heavily from the neck and telling his friend to stay with him, he hurried to call the police from a nearby telephone box. The callbox was occupied and Jones knocked on the glass asking the caller to hurry. Walter Wiggins saw that the boy was barely alive and needed urgent attention, and rather than wait for the ambulance he hurried to summon Dr Murphy who lived nearby.

Dr Murphy tried to make the young lad comfortable until the ambulance could ferry him to hospital, but at 10.20 pm he was pronounced dead on arrival. The boy was identified as ten year old Norman Yates, who had left his home on Heywood Street to run an errand for his mother. He had only been gone five minutes and must have encountered his killer almost at once. But who would want to kill a young boy?

A post-mortem showed that death had been caused by four knife wounds: three of the wounds to the chest, while the fourth, and fatal blow, had severed the neck close to the adam's apple causing a haemorrhage.

The investigation was handled by Chief Superintendent Lindsay and although nobody had seen Norman's killer as he made his getaway, a number of witnesses gave police a description of a man seen in the area shortly before the murder – aged around 20 to 30 years old, 5ft 2ins to 5ft 6ins tall, slim build, long blond hair swept back, sagging jaw – possibly with no teeth – and a prominent nose, wearing a blue suit and crepe soles and a silver wrist watch. He also had the habit of rubbing his hands together as he spoke. The wanted notice issued by the police, ended with the line: 'Two boys have already been stabbed to death in the Wigan district. Your help may prevent another boy being murdered.'

Lindsay thought that he had a likely suspect when it was learned that a patient from a Liverpool mental hospital had escaped and was believed to be heading for his home in the Wigan area. When it was learned that he matched the description of the killer the hunt was stepped up. On Tuesday afternoon he was arrested, but after satisfying the police of his innocence he was eliminated from enquiries and returned to the institution.

The hunt for the killer involved all available officers in the region with many from neighbouring towns drafted in to help. On Wednesday morning, Lindsay anounced that he urgently wished to speak to the man using the telephone box at the time of the murder as he might have seen the killer while making the call. On Thursday afternoon, after hearing of an appeal for him to come forward, postman Percy Green confirmed that he had been summoning a doctor for a relative who had been taken ill, but was unable to offer any help to the officers.

Lindsay was surprised at the lack of leads regarding his suspect, bearing in mind his visually striking features which he felt sure would betray him. Every witness in the area on the night of the murder reported seeing a blond-haired man, and each statement seemed to verify every other.

On Friday afternoon, Norman was buried at Westwood cemetery. The cortege passed slowly through Lower Ince, the streets lined with many of his young schoolmates who stood with their caps in their hands, several in tears. Numerous wreaths were piled high at the cemetery gates including one from the parents of young Billy Harmer, murdered the previous summer, and who police believed had been killed by the same person.

As the funeral ended, a rumour spread that a man had been arrested for Norman's murder and a large crowd converged on Lower Ince police station. At 8.10 pm that evening, Superintendent Lindsay announced that 23 year old Norman William Green had been cautioned and charged with the murder of Norman Yates and that he would appear at Wigan magistrates court on the following morning.

Green had been arrested at his workplace, Charlson and Sons, corn millers, on Dawber Street, Wigan, after enquiries turned up his name on more than one occasion as a likely suspect. Detective Sergeants Edmundson and Parkinson called at the factory shortly after lunch on Friday afternoon. Green was interviewed in the manager's office and both detectives were struck immediately by his close resemblance to the description of the wanted man.

He was asked to account for his movements on Easter Monday night and gave a detailed account denying being anywhere near Lower Ince. When asked why he had not come forward, as he clearly fitted the description of the wanted man, Green said it was because he 'didn't want any trouble'. When told by detectives that they did not believe his version of the night's events, Green changed his story a little, saying that he had been drinking in the Railway Hotel, Lower Ince. 'I have told you the truth now. I was in the Railway, but had nothing to do with that boy.'

Edmundson then went to Green's home on neaby Hallgate and took away a blue suit which Green admitted to wearing on Easter Monday. As the suit was being examined at the forensic laboratory, Green suddenly confessed to the murder, adding, 'I am sorry. I am very sorry for his mother. I hope she forgives me for what I have done.'

Later that Friday evening, two detectives accompanied Green back to his workplace. He directed them to a sack on the second floor where he told them they would find the murder weapon, and they later took away a wicked looking knife. 'That's the knife,' Green indicated, 'I think there will be some blood on it.'

On Saturday morning Green was questioned by Detective Inspector Davies who was still investigating the murder of William Harmer in August of the previous year, and later that morning, Chief Superintendent Lindsay announced to the press that Green was to be charged with the murder of both young boys.

What sort of man was Green? They learned that he was 23 years old, single and a native of Aberdeen, but for many years had lived with his widowed mother and elder brother in Wigan, after spending his early schooldays in and around Northumberland. He settled in Wigan in July 1940 and finished his education at the end of the war, and was working in a cotton mill when he was called up for National Service. Green was classified as Grade Two defective due to poor eyesight and opted to serve his time in the mines. In 1951 he was re-assessed by the medical board and found to be Grade Three defective with weak eyesight and a hernia. He was also thought to be emotionally unstable and was classified as unfit for National Service. Since 1951 he had been employed as a corn grinder at Charlson and Sons.

Green came before Mr Justice Oliver at Manchester Assizes in the first week of July. Although it was summertime, Green stood in the dock dressed in a fawn shirt with a green zip pullover, light coloured trousers, a sports coat and a mac. He was represented by Mr J.D. Robertson Crichton QC and pleaded not guilty.

The court then heard a contest by both counsels, one claiming that the murderer was insane and therefore not responsible for his actions, that he kept getting the urge to kill and that he couldn't fight it, the other that Green was a wicked killer who had murdered two young boys and made a failed attempt to kill a third. Parts of Green's statement were read out in court, in which he admitted the murder of Norman Yates.

'Yes, I killed him . . .' he began, saying that he had visited the Railway Hotel until 9 pm when he had left by the back door after visiting the lavatory. 'As I stood at the door I caught sight of a young boy coming down the street. I walked up the entry and the boy followed me. I turned around and asked him where I could get a glass of water. The boy said I could get one at his mother's home and I followed him across the street towards the house. We crossed the back street and I killed him there. When I killed him he screamed. I stabbed him four times.'

It was clear to the jury of ten men and two women that Green was the killer, but they had to decide if he was guilty of wilful murder, or insane as the defence claimed. The trial lasted four days and at shortly before 3 pm on Tuesday afternoon, 5th July, the jury retired to consider their verdict. They returned at 6.24 pm and asked the judge for further direction on the issue of insanity. Fifteen minutes later they returned and announced that they found Green guilty as charged.

The clerk rose to his feet. 'Norman William Green, you have been convicted of murder on the verdict of the jury. Have you anything to say why judgement of death should not be passed on you, according to law?'

'No, sir,' Green mumbled, and as the black cap was placed on Mr Justice Oliver's head and the sentence was passed, Green began to shake visibly. His mother who had sat in court throughout the trial clutching a bible, also began to weep. As the sentence ended, Green had to be assisted from the dock into the cell below. On Wednesday 27th July, 1955, Norman Green was hanged at Walton prison.

14

ONE TELL-TALE
SLIVER OF GLASS

THE MURDER OF FREDERICK GALLAGHER AT BLACKBURN, FEBRUARY 1960

Successful police work often depends upon painstaking attention to detail, and in February 1960 the murderer of Frederick Gallagher was caught with the aid of a sliver of glass less than an eighth of an inch long.

Fridays were always the busiest day of the week at the small pawnshop and general store on Eanam Road, just a few hundred yards from Blackburn railway station, as large numbers of regular customers, with wages in their pockets, came to reclaim items pawned earlier in the week.

February 12th, 1960, had been like most other Fridays for the manager of the Eanam shop, 55 year old Frederick Gallagher. Since moving from his home in Blackburn some three years earlier, Fred had developed a routine on Fridays that saw him lock up at just before 6 pm, call at the local chip shop for his tea and then meet up with a couple of old pals at Blackburn dog track before catching the late bus back to his home in Blackpool.

It was approaching midnight when his wife, Nellie, became anxious that something was wrong. It wasn't like Fred to miss the bus, he was always most careful to be at the station in good time. A call to the Ribble bus station confirmed that the bus had left on schedule and all the passengers had alighted at the depot a good hour ago.

Finally, at 2 am, Mrs Gallagher reported her husband's non-arrival home to the local police, who telegraphed their colleagues in Blackburn. The pawnshop was on a beat patrolled by Constable Leslie Bolton and a message was relayed, telling him to visit the shop.

Bolton had in fact passed the shop shortly before midnight, and as was his usual practice, he had shone his torch through the front window and tried the door handle but thought it locked.

He returned to the shop at 4 am and tried the door again. This time, having forced the handle down hard, he found that it was unlocked and had presumably been so when he had made his earlier rounds. Shining his torch into the cluttered shop, he saw spots of blood on the floor and signs of a disturbance. Edging his way inside, treading carefully as he made his way through the shop, the constable entered the small room at the back that housed the pledge counter and safe. Snapping on the light, he peered over the counter and found the body of Mr Gallagher slumped against the door. The old man had obviously been subjected to a number of blows about the head and a check of his pulse found him to be dead.

A look round the room saw that the safe was standing open and empty, evidently cleared out by whoever had attacked Mr Gallagher. Lying beside the body was a heavy iron bar, usually used to bolt the back door, and clearly visible on it were bloodstains and human hair. Mr Gallagher's pockets had been turned inside out and beside the body was his bus pass, a number of coins and his wage packet – empty. Fragments of glass, identifiable by the neck which was still in one piece as from a sterilised milk bottle, also littered the floor. It appeared that Mr Gallagher had wielded the bottle in an attempt to defend himself.

By mid afternoon Detective Superintendent Jim Davies and Detective Sergeant Harry Heavens had arrived from Scotland Yard to take over the investigation. A press conference was arranged for that evening and the initial enquiries centred on the identity of a number of people seen in the busy shop late Friday afternoon. There was also the possibility that he had been killed by someone from the dog-track who knew he was fond of betting and often carried a lot of money. With no obvious suspects, this was an investigation that would rely upon painstaking and thorough investigation.

Mr Fred Fielding, the managing director of the chain of pawnshops, told officers that he had called at the Eanam shop at 5 pm and delivered Gallagher's wages of £8 13s 1d. He had also carried two bags each containing a bundle of notes amounting to over £100 to be used as a cash reserve and float. In total over £180 was missing from the safe, along with Gallagher's wages and gold watch with an expanding bracelet.

Fielding had noticed a man sitting in the pledge room and gave a

The pawn shop where the murder took place. *(Lancashire Evening Telegraph)*

rough description of him. Several other customers also mentioned the mysterious man seated in the shop. He had told one witness that he was waiting for his wife who was using a nearby launderette, but police learned he must have been in the shop for well over an hour.

Mrs Livesy, a local shopkeeper, told detectives that shortly after 5.30 pm that Friday afternoon, Fred Gallagher had called at the shop and purchased two fruit flans instead of his usual one. When officers checked the room they found no sign of the flans but did find two foil wrappers in the rubbish basket. A pathologist later confirmed that Gallagher had not eaten a flan that afternoon.

More and more witnesses came forward describing the man seen both inside the shop, and in the street outside shortly afterwards. He was aged around 30 years old, with a long pointed nose, prominent protruding ears, very thick dark hair and dressed scruffily – like a layabout. He was also said to be hungry looking and wearing a dark suit and a discoloured dark raincoat.

Several people mentioned that the man appeared to be talking to Gallagher until they had entered the shop when he then lapsed into silence. Davies also learned that the last sighting of Fred Gallagher was at shortly after 6 pm, and a man was seen running down a nearby street at 6.15 pm. The latter was said to be holding a bunch of keys and in a great hurry.

Who was this mystery man? Detectives reasoned that he was presumably a man out of work, possibly a down and out sheltering from the cold. Had the kindly old man offered his killer warmth and, remembering the purchase of the flans, perhaps bought him something to eat?

On Friday, 19th February, Frederick Gallagher was buried at Carleton cemetery, in the presence of his family, his many friends, and a number of senior detectives.

Detectives meanwhile studied the pieces of broken bottle found beside the body. Slivers of glass showed traces of blood and these were collected together and sent to the forensic laboratory at Preston where they were examined by Chief Inspector Louis Allen. Using high-powered microscopes, Allen was able to match up the pieces and gradually reconstruct the bottle like a jigsaw. Allen pointed out to the Scotland Yard detectives the lines of striation on the glass, caused during manufacture by the tremendous heat and as individual to each bottle as a fingerprint.

On Thursday, 25th February, 1960, the routine and exhaustive investigation paid off. An officer on a visit to the Globe works in nearby Accrington learned that on the day of the murder the foreman had laid a man off for bad time-keeping.

Mihaly Pocze was a 25 year old Hungarian refugee who lived with his wife and young child on Mowbray Avenue, less than a mile from the pawnshop. Officers from Blackburn CID visited the house and found no sign of Pocze. They learned that he had left his wife in Blackburn on the day of the murder and had probably gone to South Wales where he was friendly with a number of Hungarians.

The search was on. A watch was placed on all ports and airports while detectives travelled down to Hirwaun near Merthyr Tydfil, and made enquiries amongst the local Hungarians. They learned that Pocze was the son of a Hungarian prison warden and was probably trying to raise funds to return to his native Budapest. He fitted the description given by the witnesses and police were told that he sported a distinctive tattoo on the back of his right hand. Investigations in Hirwaun also recovered a gold wrist watch which was later identified as belonging to Mr Gallagher. Pocze had sold the watch to a fellow Hungarian before leaving the town. Police were

Mihaly Pocze. *(Lancashire Evening Telegraph)*

tipped off that he had probably made for London.

On Saturday, 27th February, Pocze was arrested at a house in Chelsea. Detective Superintendent Davies spoke to Pocze at Chelsea police station and told him he was making enquiries concerning the murder of a man in a Blackburn pawnshop. Pocze replied, 'What is pawnshop? Not in shop. Who see me?'

He claimed that on the day of the murder he had spent the day in bed before catching the seven o'clock train to London. His wife could not confirm his alibi as she was visiting her mother on the Friday afternoon. Davies told the Hungarian that he had a witness who claimed that Pocze had told him he was carrying over £200 when he left Blackburn, but Pocze was adamant he had never made this claim. At 10.34 pm that Saturday night, Pocze was formally charged with murder and replied, 'Not guilty'. He was remanded for a week pending further enquiries.

With a man in custody it was now down to proving the case against him. Officers at the Preston forensic laboratory had found a number of prints on the milk bottle. These matched those of Pocze but there was a slight snag. The dairy which had supplied the bottle, the Palatine Dairy, had employed Pocze several years earlier, so it was possible, although highly unlikely, that his prints could have got onto the bottle during this time.

Blood found in the bathroom at Pocze's house matched that of the victim – group O – but it also matched the suspect. Pocze, however, claimed that he had not cut himself recently but his wife had. A check on her blood found it to be group A.

Pocze was put up for identification and was pointed out by several witnesses as the man seen in the pawnshop on the afternoon of the murder. A witness testified that he had bought the stolen watch from Pocze in Wales and Mrs Spencer, Pocze's mother-in-law, testified that a number of items thought to have been taken from the shop and found at Pocze's house, did not belong to the prisoner or his wife.

The most damning evidence against Pocze was spotted by a sharp-eyed detective examining the bathroom at his house. Nestled in a crack below the sink was a tiny sliver of glass. Less than an eighth of an inch long, and barely half as wide, the tiny blood-speckled segment fitted perfectly into the reconstructed bottle at the forensic laboratory.

Satisfied that they had the right man, Mihaly Pocze was charged with Capital Murder (in the furtherance of theft, and therefore liable to the death penalty) and committed for trial at Lancaster Assizes.

At the subsequent trial, held before Mr Justice Hinchcliffe, Pocze's defence counsel chose the only option open to them in the face of overwhelming evidence, and asked for a verdict of guilty but insane. Mr J. Robertson Crichton QC, defending Pocze, claimed that at the time of the attack the accused was suffering from an abnormality of the mind which subsequently impaired his responsibility. The defence asked that the court find him guilty of the lesser charge of manslaughter. Evidence that Pocze was a high-grade mental defective was contested by the Crown who produced two doctors to refute the claims, both of whom had had the chance to study the prisoner's behaviour at length while he was awaiting trial.

It took the jury less than an hour to make their decision and Pocze was sentenced to death. His appeal was heard before Mr Justice Hilbery on 25th July, and this too was rejected. Then, on 1st August, 1960, eleven days before he was due to hang, the Home Secretary announced that he had spared the Hungarian's life. Doubts had evidently remained concerning Pocze's mental state though, as was the practice, no reason was given for the decision to reprieve the prisoner. However, nothing could detract from the success of the police investigation and the forensic evidence – especially that tiny sliver of glass.

15

MOSAIC OF MURDER

THE MURDER OF ISABELLA CROSS AT MANCHESTER, MAY 1962

In 1962, two years after the successful investigation into the death of Frederick Gallagher in Blackburn, Detective Chief Inspector Allen at the Preston forensic laboratory was again to show that a sliver of glass could prove a man guilty of murder.

It was on another Friday, 4th May, 1962, that Mrs Isabella Cross was battered to death in her little sweet and tobacconist's shop on the corner of Hulme Hall Lane and Iron Street, Miles Platting.

At 4.25 pm, Mrs Cross signed the delivery note for a consignment of cigarettes. Five minutes later, nine year old schoolgirl Stephanie Howarth called into the shop and when no one came to serve her she called out. No reply. She repeated the call and at the same time stood on tiptoe and peeped over the counter. Lying in a heap beneath the opened till was the body of the shopkeeper.

Stephanie rushed back to her house in tears shouting, 'Come quick, Auntie Belle's been killed!' Her sister and a neighbour went to the shop and saw the body on the floor lying in a mixture of blood and lemonade. Fragments of glass were scattered around and it appeared the killer had battered Isabella to death with one of the mineral bottles that had stood beside the counter.

Officers from Manchester CID, led by Detective Chief Superintendent Eric Cunningham, arrived at the scene and started their investigation. From the outset it seemed certain robbery was the motive and that the kindly old lady had been murdered for the contents of the till. A car was sent to fetch Isabella's husband David home from his job at a nearby Royal Ordnance factory, and in tears he told the police that the thief must have gotten away with the afternoon's takings. It would not have been a great deal of money.

It was soon clear that Mrs Cross had been battered to death with a number of one-pint mineral bottles; her clothing and the floor were completely soaked in lemonade. Glass fragments covered the shop floor, and the presence of five bottle tops indicated the exact number used. Some small change was lying around and the till was open. One sharp-eyed officer spotted a bloodstained fingerprint on a sliver of glass lying close to the door.

It appeared that the killer was not satisfied with the contents of the till because the connecting door leading from the shop, which was always kept closed, was ajar, and it looked as if he had rummaged through the desk in the sitting room. One of the drawers had been pulled out and its contents scattered across the carpet.

The doors from the sitting room to the kitchen and from the kitchen to the backyard were open, as was the back gate leading into the street. Evidently the man had made his escape through the back, presumably after hearing the bell when Stephanie entered the shop. Chief Superintendent Cunningham later remarked that it was fortunate Stephanie had arrived when she did, for he felt sure if she had called a minute earlier and disturbed the intruder, he would probably have killed her too.

A large number of fingerprints were found on the premises, as they would have expected given the nature of the business, but fortunately the police got a lucky break.

David Cross told them that he had recently decorated inside the shop and other downstairs rooms, and this included painting the living room door, which he had done just three days previously. On the edge of this door was a clear set of prints which did not belong to either the victim or her husband. Cross told Cunningham there had been no visitors since he had completed the decorating, so it was surmised that the fingerprints belonged to the killer. To preserve the prints, Cunningham had the door removed from its hinges and taken to the Lancashire police headquarters at Preston, where scores of experts combed through the extensive files for a matching print. The particles of glass were also photographed and sent to Preston, in the vain hope that they would yield more clues.

The detectives considered the killer. Cunningham thought him likely to be a local man, perhaps someone who passed by on his way home from work. He reasoned that the ferocity of the crime bore the hallmark of a man used to violence, and who therefore probably had a criminal record, and the chances were that his prints would be on file. While the fingerprint staff worked round the clock, Cunningham ordered a house to house search of all likely suspects in the area.

A week after the murder Cunningham thought he had his man. A stranger seen entering the yard behind the shop was taken into custody, and faint traces of glass were found on the soles of his shoes. Under interrogation he confessed to the murder. The man gave detailed knowledge of the inside of the shop but it was later found that his prints did not match the ones found on the door or the glass, and nothing he said about the crime could not have been gleaned from reading the newspapers. After a reprimand for wasting police time he was released. A frequent source of frustration for officers investigating a murder case is having to deal with cranks who waste their time and effort with false confessions.

At the Preston headquarters, Detective Chief Inspector Allen was given the mammoth task of reassembling the bottles. With a myriad of glass particles and a tube of glue he set about the mosaic. He had of course encountered a similar problem two years earlier when he and his colleagues at the laboratory had been asked to help Blackburn police identify glass from the Eanam pawnshop, but this case involved a lot more work. Some of the larger pieces matched up quite easily, and with the aid of a microscope Allen was able to piece together other fragments using striation.

Copies of the killer's prints had been sent to Scotland Yard and other police departments and three weeks after the murder detectives in Edinburgh turned up a matching print.

Furnished with a name, Cunningham now had to locate the suspect. The wanted man was James Smith, a 26 year old Scotsman, living with his wife and two children at 4 Corfe Street, Beswick, Manchester. Police were alarmed to find that the area was due for demolition and many of the houses were boarded up ready for the workmen to move in. Fortunately, number 4 was still occupied.

For the last year, Smith had been employed as a rubber moulder at Ferguson Shiers Ltd, on Cheetham Street, Failsworth, on the outskirts of Manchester. Smith worked shifts, and police learned that the day shift finished at noon on Fridays.

On the day of the murder Smith had been on the day shift. He had finished work as normal and went to the pub with his workmates. Edward Hunt, with whom Smith usually travelled part of the way home, told officers that on that afternoon he had left the pub at 2.45 pm, while Smith was still drinking. Normally they would travel home on the Failsworth to Manchester city centre bus, and Smith would alight on the corner of Hulme Hall Lane, a quarter of a mile from the shop.

From the bus stop Smith could then either catch another bus that would take him to his front door, or he could walk, a journey that normally took around 20 minutes. Hunt added that on Sunday 6th May, Smith had called on him sporting a plaster on his right hand. He told Hunt he had cut himself on a spike.

Detectives planned to arrest Smith at home on Saturday 26th May, but they had to be sure he was there. One false move and the prey could escape. Cunningham decided not to risk a visit until he was certain his man was inside, and a stake out ensured there were no comings or goings at the house throughout the night. At 8 am next morning, Cunningham and Detective Inspector Tom Butcher, his second-in-command, knocked on the front door. Smith readily admitted knowing the shop where the old lady was killed. 'Everybody knows it!' he claimed. 'It's been on television and in the papers for the last fortnight.'

Smith strongly denied ever visiting the shop but admitted he had walked past it on his way home from work on the day of the murder. It must have been about 4.20 pm, he said, because he was home at 4.30 pm when the insurance man had called. John Hamilton, the insurance agent in question, regularly called at Corfe Street on Friday afternoons, but he told detectives that he did not visit number 4 until at least 4.45 pm and he could not be sure if Smith was at home.

Cunningham ordered a thorough search of the house. A vacuum cleaner was inserted down the side of the sofa and revealed a piece of glass similar to those in the reconstructed bottles. Under the microscope it was clear the glass could only have come from one of the bottles used in the attack.

Satisfied Smith was their man, he was arrested and taken to Mill Street police station and later that afternoon charged with the Capital Murder of Mrs Isabella Cross. Detective Inspector Butcher sat with Smith minutes after he had been charged. The prisoner turned to Butcher and joked, 'I'll bet you a fiver I never hang.' Not holding out much hope for the prisoner's chances of escaping the hangman, Butcher replied, 'You're on.'

James Smith stood trial at Liverpool Assizes before Mr Justice Stable in October 1962. The presence of his fingerprints on the living room door proved he had been on the shop premises but that alone did not prove he was there at the time of the crime. It was the sliver of glass found at his home, identical to particles from the shop and which fitted perfectly in the reconstructed bottles, that placed him there at the time of the murder.

On the afternoon of 19th October, the judge donned a black cap and the hushed courtroom heard him pronounce sentence of death on Smith. Two weeks later his appeal was heard before Lord Chief Justice Gorman and Mr Justice Salmon. They concurred with the original sentence and could find no reason to allow the appeal. The Home Secretary was also petitioned but he too was unswayed, and decided the law must take its course.

On Wednesday morning, 28th November, James Smith was hanged at Strangeways prison, Manchester. Later that morning Detectives Cunningham and Butcher visited the prison to identify the body. Looking down at the body in the mortuary, Butcher took little comfort in the fact that he had won the bet he knew he would never collect.

16

THE GOOD SAMARITAN

**THE MURDER OF FLORENCE CHADWICK AT BURNLEY,
OCTOBER 1967**

Motiveless murder is usually one of the hardest types of crime for detectives to solve. With no obvious suspect and few clues, it is often down to pure chance that the guilty are brought to justice. The pointless killing of an elderly lady in Burnley during the autumn of 1967 was fortunately one of the rare cases in which the police had the case wrapped up within 24 hours.

Sixty year old Florence Chadwick, a kindly widow who lived with her youngest son Arthur at 106 Every Street, Burnley, worked as a barmaid at the Concord bar in Burnley town centre. It was the policy of the bar to provide staff with a taxi after closing time and shortly before midnight on Friday, 13th October, 1967, Florrie, as she was known to her friends, bought a bottle of stout and asked the taxi to drop her off at Sandygate, as she planned to share the bottle with her friend, 78 year old Annie Cocker.

Mrs Cocker lived at 27 Lord Street, in an area awaiting slum clearance by Burnley Corporation. Her house and one other were the only ones that had not been boarded up ready for demolition. The old lady was partially disabled and Mrs Chadwick, a friend for close on 40 years, was a frequent visitor who would run errands and do other chores.

Florrie arrived at the house at a few minutes after midnight, and the ladies shared the stout and chatted for around three quarters of an hour before Florrie set off for the short walk to her own home. Twenty minutes later, just as Annie was preparing for bed, she heard a faint cry from the street outside. The voice seemed to be calling her name and opening the door she saw Florrie lying face down on the pavement.

Annie shrieked at the sight of her friend in distress, and called out for help. Two young men walking on the opposite side of the road rushed over and while one administered first aid, the other ran to fetch help.

The old lady's scream had echoed through the deserted streets and was heard by a chip shop owner, Mrs Joan Phillips, who was unwinding after a busy night behind the counter at her shop at 93 Piccadilly Road, a hundred yards away from Mrs Cocker's house. Walking back into the shop area, she saw a young man she recognised as her next door neighbour, running across the road, and as he approached his own front door he dropped something that made a distinctly metallic sound as it struck the hard ground. Unseen in her by now darkened shop, she saw the youth enter his house and close the door behind him. She thought nothing more of it and returned to her cup of cocoa.

Florence Chadwick. *(Burnley Express)*

By the time police had arrived at Lord Street Mrs Chadwick had succumbed to her injuries and a murder enquiry was set up. At first light a team of officers combed the area aided by police dogs, and they quickly located the old lady's lower set of dentures, a pair of spectacles and a key ring. A police car with a loudspeaker patrolled the area appealing for anyone with information to come forward and newspaper placards were posted outside every newsagent with a similar message.

A post-mortem was held later that morning and Dr Charles St Hill, the pathologist, told detectives that the killer had stabbed the old lady twice: once in the lower back which had penetrated one and a half inches deep, and the second time in the left side of the chest, a four inch deep cut which had punctured the aorta. A third cut was found in her handbag which she had probably used to fend off a further attack.

The police set up their headquarters in the concert room at the local police station as teams of officers began the rounds of door to door routine enquiries. These were the first steps taken in most murder investigations and they instantly paid off.

An officer called at the chip shop on Piccadilly Road and interviewed the owner. She mentioned seeing her neighbour, 19 year old Douglas Gardner, running down the street away from the Sandygate area. Furnished with this vital tip off, Detective Inspector Slater and Detective Sergeant Johnson from the regional crime squad, visited Gardner at his home later that Saturday afternoon.

He said that he had heard of the murder from his mother who had told him about it after she had returned from shopping just before dinner. Gardner was asked about his movements on the previous evening and said that he had finished work at 7.30 and arrived home about ten minutes later. He added that he was an apprentice with a firm of bookbinders. After a wash and change, he had sat down and watched an episode of *Danger Man* on television before calling at a friend's house and together they went out into town.

Continuing, he told Johnson that they visited the Casino Club in the town where they watched a beauty contest, and after drinking around five or six pints of 'black and tan' he left the club with another friend, Michael Wilson, at around 12.30 am. They walked to the bus station and chatted while queuing for a taxi. Tired of waiting for a cab, Gardner decided to walk home and arrived there at 1.15 am. He claimed that he did not see anyone while walking home nor did he hear any noise, and when he reached home he went straight to bed. Asked if this was a true account, Gardner pondered for a second before replying, 'Yes, as far as I know.'

While Gardner was giving the account of his movements, Detective Inspector Slater was searching through his room. He noticed a large cupboard which was secured by a padlock and chain, the key to which he found in the pocket of a jacket hanging behind the door. The inspector opened the cupboard and found a sheathed knife covered with what looked like blood. He showed the knife to Gardner and asked him if he could identify it. Gardner admitted that the knife belonged to him but claimed that he had got it when he was in the Scouts and had never carried it.

While Gardner was being taken to the police station, an officer was sent to question Michael Wilson about his movements the previous evening. Wilson confirmed most of the alibi except for one vital point. Asked what time they left the club, Wilson replied, 'About 11.30 pm', a good hour before the time Gardner claimed.

Back at the station Gardner was interviewed again; this time Inspector Reavely of the Burnley Borough Force took notes while Detective Inspector Parkinson asked the questions.

DI Parkinson: Would you care to tell me what you did last night?
Gardner: I finished work at 7.30, watched TV, went to my mate's house, and from there to the Casino. I left the Casino about 1 am, and went to the bus station to get a taxi. I didn't get one so I walked home.
DI Parkinson: You left the Casino before 1 am, Wilson stated he was home before midnight. You were seen running into your home after one o'clock, and you dropped something on to the road.
Gardner: I didn't drop anything. I wasn't running.
DI Parkinson: Why don't you tell me the truth?
Gardner: I think I did it but I don't remember.
DI Parkinson: What do you mean?
Gardner: I vaguely remember.

Gardner then made a statement in which he admitted the attack: 'After leaving Wilson I remember going home. I took my coat off then put it back on. I remember hitting her and had the knife in my hand. I stabbed her and it were in Sandygate. I didn't know I had killed her until my mother came home from the shop.'

He admitted that he felt bad about the attack, even more so when he learned that the victim was the mother of one of his former classmates. He concluded the statement by saying, 'I would like to apologise if I can.'

On 12th February, 1968, he stood in the dock before Mr Justice Fenton Atkinson, and entered a plea of not guilty to the murder of Florence Chadwick. The trial lasted five hours and ended when the jury returned a guilty verdict. Mr Justice Atkinson sentenced the prisoner to life imprisonment and he was ushered from the dock.

Why did a 19 year old, perfectly sane young man, with previous good character, suddenly resort to murder? No motive was ever suggested or proven. The victim had been carrying a small amount of money but that was still in her possession after the crime. Although the killer knew Mrs Chadwick's son, there was no evidence that he knew Mrs Chadwick, as he claimed. It has been suggested that after witnessing the beauty contest, he became sexually frustrated, which combined with his drunken state drove him to kill the first female he saw as he walked home alone.

Unfortunately for Mrs Chadwick – the Good Samaritan, returning from comforting an elderly friend – she happened to be in the wrong place at the wrong time. Fortunately for the police, Mrs Phillips, in her small fish and chip shop, was in the right place at the right time.

17

UNWELCOME ADVANCES

THE MURDER OF ALAN KENYON AT HARWOOD, DECEMBER 1970

Alan Kenyon led a double life. To his neighbours he was an easy going, hard working, pleasant free-spending bachelor, but unknown to all but his closest friends, he was also a homosexual. By day, he was often seen out and about enjoying early retirement at the age of just 37, but by night he frequented numerous bars and gay clubs, often taking strangers back to his picturesque cottage at Harwood, a modern sprawling village on the northern tip of Bolton.

On Sunday, 14th December, 1970, a local farmer and long time friend of Kenyon's, called at the cottage on Lea Gate Lane after Alan had failed to turn up for the usual Sunday lunch and pint at The Seven Stars, a few hundred yards away.

Approaching the cottage he saw Alan's blue sports car standing in the drive and trying the front door he found it unlocked. 'Alan! Is anyone home?' he shouted as he entered the porch. Receiving no reply he entered the living room and called out again. He turned on the light as the heavy drapes were still drawn, and the room was in total darkness. Kenyon's friend walked through to the bedroom and knocked on the door. Still no answer.

'Alan?' he shouted and opening the bedroom door, he recoiled in horror. Lying on the bed, naked except for a pair of socks, was the body of Alan Kenyon. The white top sheet was stained a deep crimson by the blood that had seeped from a number of lacerations to the head, and lying at the foot of the bed was a heavy brass poker.

Officers from Lancashire CID, led by Detective Chief Superintendent Alfred Collins, sealed off the house and, after setting up a murder headquarters at the nearby Liberal Club, they immediately

103

Alan Kenyon's 'local' – the Seven Stars.

began house to house enquiries in the village. Collins soon learned of Kenyon's double life and this presented him with a problem; the homosexual community were often reluctant to get involved with the police and this investigation was to be no different. The police did learn from other sources that Kenyon had sold a diamond watch for over £200 on the Saturday afternoon and had received £10 in cash and a cheque for the remainder. A search of the house failed to locate the cheque.

In the living room of the house they found three whisky glasses, a sign that he had obviously had company on the previous evening. Police patched together the victim's last movements and learned that he was last seen in his dark blue Triumph GT6 sports car at the junction of Tonge Moor Road and Crompton Way, facing towards Bradshaw. He was returning home after dropping off a young boy with whom he had spent the last couple of hours.

Next morning, a post-mortem was held by Dr Woodcock at Bolton Royal Infirmary. The doctor confirmed that the injuries had almost certainly been caused by the poker found beside the body, and it appeared that the blows had been struck while the man was lying down on the bed. There were bruises on the hands and arms as though the victim had made a last desperate attempt to fend off the attack. Dr Woodcock said that Kenyon had survived the attack for about two hours and that death was due to cerebral haemorrhage caused by repeated blows to the head and neck.

Police pondered the motive. It seemed at first that robbery was the probable cause, especially as the cheque was missing, but later when the safe in the bedroom was opened the cheque was located. Also missing from the house were two coats, and detectives believed the killer might have taken these to cover up bloodstains on his clothes.

They assumed that after having dropped off his friend, Kenyon had either picked up another man or had perhaps telephoned the killer and invited him to call.

With over 90 officers assigned to the investigation, Collins concentrated on two clues taken from the house. One was a cigarette lighter shaped like an automatic pistol, which friends claimed did not belong to the victim, the other was a white string vest. This seemed a major clue as it bore the name-tag 'David G. Whalley'. The vest obviously did not belong to Mr Kenyon and a check on the files at the Criminal Record Office failed to turn up anyone of that name.

The name-tag was the type used by institutions like the military and officers were detailed to check through records of any likely user of such a tag. It was an enormous task and many officers were assigned to methodically work through the various organisations.

Meanwhile, detectives in Bolton learned that on the Sunday morning a driver had given a man a lift on Crompton Way, a couple of miles away from the cottage, and dropped him off on Chorley New Road, believing him to be heading for Atherton. He gave a good description of the man whom he said had dark curly hair with long bushy side-boards, a full face, high cheek bones and dark eyebrows, aged about 19 years old and about five foot ten inches tall.

There were literally dozens of fingerprints in the house and when Collins learned that Kenyon was very house-proud and fond of showing neighbours around, he wondered if there was a single person in Harwood who had not been inside the house. Detectives also checked through the victim's numerous confidential telephone numbers in the hope that someone could throw light on the investigation.

Four days after the murder Collins and his officers had the break-through they had been searching for. While enquiries continued slowly in Bolton, the trail led to Preston and an unsolved robbery from the previous springtime.

'David G. Whalley' was found to be a House Surgeon at Preston Royal Infirmary, and the vest was among a number of items he had reported stolen from the hospital laundry sometime around 6th March in the previous year. The description of the wanted man, and the theft of laundry at Preston, led officers to check up on the whereabouts of a convicted criminal currently on the run from Wakefield prison.

On Tuesday, 22nd December, 1970, just when it seemed as if the officers would have to cancel their Christmas leave, they had a man in custody. Acting on information received, Detective Chief Inspector Ian Hunter of Blackburn's Number 2 Task Force called at a house belonging to 22 year old Gordon Leonard Lee on Aqueduct Street, Preston. His wife, Florence Lee, opened the door and admitted the officers. The house was searched and Lee was found hiding in a small cabinet under the kitchen sink.

'Well, you've got to try, haven't you,' he said to the officer as he was placed under arrest. He was taken back to Bolton and under interrogation he admitted the attack.

'All right, I'll give it to you straight,' he said when questioned at Astley Bridge police station. 'This is how it happened. I had been drinking in town and was walking up Blackburn Road where I intended to spend the night with friends. A man in a two-seater sports car stopped and offered me a lift. It was raining and I accepted. He invited me back to his house for a drink and again I accepted. He made advances and asked me to stop the night, but I didn't think anything of it at first. I had got my shirt off when he made a grab at me. I pushed him away, but he would not stop, so I hit him with the poker. When I left he was still breathing and I didn't know he was dead until I read it in the papers.'

It seemed clear to detectives that Lee was probably hoping for a manslaughter charge, emphasising the provocation on a number of occasions. When questioned about the stolen coats he admitted that he had sold them; one in Buckley, the other in Blyth, Northumberland. He said that after returning to Preston he decided to 'jump ship' and fled, first to Buckley in Flintshire, where he sold one of the coats, then to North Shields from where he planned to sail to Europe. For some reason he decided to return to Preston and it was while he was at home he was arrested.

Gordon Lee stood trial for murder at Manchester Assizes before Mr Justice Cusack in May 1971. He pleaded not guilty to the murder of Alan Kenyon but admitted the theft of two coats.

Gordon Lee as sketched in court. *(Bolton Evening News)*

He reiterated his plea of manslaughter and the court heard how Kenyon had made unwelcome advances which he fended off by hitting him with the poker. The prosecution's claim, backed up by medical evidence, that many of the blows had been delivered while the man was lying on the bed seemed to contradict this account and when the jury came to weigh up the verdict, after three days of evidence, they found Lee guilty of murder.

When the judge had passed the sentence of life imprisonment, the court was told that Lee was on the run from prison where he was serving four years for aggravated burglary. He also had numerous convictions for violent crime.

Thus Alan Kenyon, the man whose door was always open to his friends and neighbours, died because he made unwelcome advances to the wrong kind of guest.

18

FOR JUSTICE AND LAW

THE MURDER OF SUPERINTENDENT GERALD RICHARDSON
AT BLACKPOOL, AUGUST 1971

Police officers face danger every day as they go about their ordinary duties, but in August 1971 Superintendent Gerald Richardson paid the ultimate price as he faced, unarmed, a desperate thief with a loaded shotgun.

Bank Holiday Monday, 23rd August, 1971, promised to be a scorcher, and inside hotels and guest houses along Blackpool's seafront holidaymakers were finishing their breakfasts and planning the day ahead. It was the height of the season and business was good all along the Golden Mile as folk from all corners of the country flocked to catch the sun at their favourite holiday spot.

Also in Blackpool, but for a very different reason, were five men who by lunchtime had turned a quiet corner of the town into something resembling a scene from a gangster movie.

Preston's jeweller's shop on the Strand, a narrow one-way street a mere pebble throw from the promenade at the North Shore, had just opened for business when four masked men burst in. While one held the staff at gunpoint, forcing them to lie face down on the carpet, the others quickly, and with ruthless efficiency, stripped the window displays of rings, watches and expensive jewels.

Unbeknown to the gang, Joseph Lammond, the shop manager, was in the stock room when the raid began, and he wasted no time in pushing the alarm button. The raid was over in less than two minutes, the alarm sending the men rushing into the street, where they dived into a getaway car.

As the last of the raiders left the shop he was intercepted by Ronald Gale, a passing fire brigade officer, one of a number of people who had been attracted by the commotion. Mr Gale bravely tried to detain the raider but was knocked to the ground, receiving a blow to the

Superintendent Gerald Richardson. *(Newspix)*

head from the butt of the man's gun.

A dark green two-litre Triumph estate car roared into life and sped from the shop, scattering the crowd of holidaymakers as a police patrol car turned into the street. Onlookers stared in horror as the rear window of the Triumph opened and the barrel of a gun was thrust out. A hail of gunfire was aimed at the pursuing panda car as the Triumph raced up Queen Street and turned into Dickson Road, near the North Station.

Other patrol cars converged on the getaway car and half a mile down the road one of them was able to ram the Triumph as it turned into Clifford Road. Unable to restart the car, the gang were forced to abandon the vehicle, and with guns blazing they made off on foot as officers closed in. One of the gang ran down an alley where he found himself confronted by Superintendent Gerald Richardson and Inspector Eddie Gray. He pointed the gun at Richardson who blocked his path.

'Don't be silly, son,' the Superintendent said, taking a step closer. Two shots rang out, and the officer slumped to the ground mortally wounded.

The gunman ran back up the alley, rejoining the gang, who now fled into Cheltenham Road where they commandeered a butcher's van, shooting and wounding another officer, PC Walker, before driving off at high speed. Panda cars chased the van into Carshalton Road where they forced it to crash into a wall. Two of the gang climbed into a grey Morris 1000 van and this time they were able to escape from the ensuing chase.

Officers arrested three of the robbers and as news of the shooting quickly spread, detectives from Blackpool CID realised they had a major incident on their hands. One officer lay dead, and another two patrolmen had suffered gunshot injuries. The gang had also stolen over £100,000 worth of jewellery, although much of this was recovered from the abandoned Triumph getaway car. They did have three men under arrest, but the killer of Superintendent Richardson was still at large.

Road blocks were set up in and around the town – a large police presence causing traffic to crawl through the maze of cones and questioning officers – but the two men still managed to slip the net.

On the following morning three of the raiders appeared in court at Blackpool; 43 year old Dennis George Bond of Clapham stood alongside John Patrick Spry, 37, of Streatham Hill, and Glasgow born Thomas Flannigan, 43, living in Hackney. They were each charged with robbing Joseph Lammond of an unknown number of watches and rings, and remanded in custody for a week.

Descriptions of the two wanted men were issued. One was described as aged between 34 and 36 years old, 5ft 10ins tall, with short dark hair and a southern accent. The other was said to be aged around 30 years old, 5ft 9ins, and stocky, with a moustache and Scottish accent. A press conference called on Tuesday afternoon named the two: one was Frederick Joseph Sewell, aged 30, of Brixton, the other they only knew as 'Doug', who was described as having a Mexican 'Pancho' style moustache.

It was rumoured amongst the underworld that the men had gone to ground in south London and 200 detectives, from both the Flying Squad and Regional Crime Squad, scoured nightclubs, hotels and flats in pursuit. Officers were issued with firearms and members of the public were warned not to approach the wanted men.

A search of Blackpool uncovered a stolen Ford Capri with false number plates. It had been abandoned outside a flat on Cocker Street, which was later found to have been rented by Sewell and a woman a few days before the murder. Inside the car were shotgun cartridges, a loaded revolver, a leather case and a first aid kit. The villains were obviously prepared for any eventuality.

A watch was kept on any known associates of Sewell, who police believed to be the leader of the gang. He was formerly a pig breeder on a large farm at Orpington, Kent, but had latterly concentrated on buying and selling motor cars from a showroom in Brixton. Acting on a tip off, detectives raided a farmhouse after a reported sighting of Sewell, and spoke to Mrs Irene Jermain, who lived with Sewell and their children in a large house at Redhill, Surrey. Mrs Jermain denied seeing him since before the Bank Holiday.

On Thursday, 26th August, while enquiries went on down south, the funeral of the murdered officer took place in Blackpool. Described as an officer who led from the front, 38 year old Superintendent Gerald Irving Richardson was married, but had no children. With over 20 years service in the force, he had three commendations for bravery, and at the time of the murder was the highest ranking police officer to be killed on duty.

So respected was he that the whole town came to a standstill. Over 100,000 people lined the route as the cortege slowly passed within yards of the spot where he was gunned down. Over 400 officers lined the route, while 300 more joined the procession, which was led by eleven mounted policemen and the police band. The flag on Blackpool tower flew at half-mast and shop assistants were given time off to watch the procession, standing in crowds which at some places were as much as 20 deep.

At almost the same time Superintendent Richardson was being laid to rest at the town's Layton Cemetery, one of the two wanted men was being taken into custody. Charles Haynes, 'Doug', was arrested near Leamington Spa and returned to Blackpool to help with enquiries.

Police reasoned that the men must have had help to slip through the road block on the day of the incident, and within a week they had three people in custody charged with 'intent to impede the apprehension and prosecution' of the wanted men. Mrs Irene Jermain was charged with driving the men out of Blackpool; it had been found that it was she (and Sewell) who had rented the flat in Blackpool and it was to here the men had returned after the murder, and from where the journey home began. Mrs Barbara Palmer, the

111

Funeral of Superintendent Richardson. *(Lancashire Evening Post)*

mother of one of Sewell's children, and Eugene Kerrigan, an employee of Sewell's at the Brixton garage, were both charged with supplying him with a change of clothes and driving him around London in search of a 'safe house'. Kerrigan was arrested carrying a large sum of money – destined for Sewell – but despite police pressure he refused to reveal the whereabouts of his employer.

When the two women were remanded in custody at a special sitting of the Blackpool court a week after the murder, police learned how Sewell had outsmarted them in making his getaway. While efforts had been concentrated on the main southbound roads out of town, the getaway car had in fact gone north, taking a number of secondary roads through the Fylde countryside, up as far as the Lakes where it then headed east through Tebay, joining the A1 in Yorkshire, where the journey south commenced.

Teams of detectives with metal detectors combed the roadsides along the supposed route, in search of any discarded weapons or jewellery, while the *Daily Mirror* put up a reward of £10,000 for any information that would lead to Sewell's arrest.

Frederick Joseph Sewell. *(Newspix)*

Reported sightings of Sewell, who had become 'Public Enemy Number One', were a daily occurrence and more than one innocent man was the subject of a police ambush after a tip off; but despite intensive police work, which included infiltrating the underworld, they were still no nearer to finding Sewell. Detective Superintendent Mounsey was convinced that Sewell had slipped the net and was probably on the Continent, possibly Scandinavia, but reports of supposed sightings in England still continued to flood in.

On 30th September, a fund raised for the murdered officer closed after collecting over £14,000, money which was to be split between Superintendent Richardson's widow and the police benevolent fund.

It was another tip off that was to lead Mounsey to the wanted man. Word reached him that Sewell was hiding in a north London flat and at first light on the morning of 7th October, a team of 40 detectives waited outside a house on Birnam Road, Holloway, for the signal to move in. The street was shrouded in fog and visibility was down to

113

less then 20 yards, as Mounsey entered the terraced house and made for the first floor flat.

On the signal from Mounsey, the door was broken down and Sewell was found lying in bed. He made a vain attempt to reach a shotgun lying in a box under the mattress before being placed under arrest. Two others were also arrested, Panayiotis Panayiotou, a 25 year old Cypriot, and Nistra Stavrou; both charged with harbouring a wanted man. Later that morning a convoy of speeding police cars set off for Blackpool where Sewell joined the other members of the gang. The 45 day manhunt had come to an end.

Sewell was hissed and jeered at as he was bundled through the back door of Blackpool police station later that afternoon. It transpired that he had been hiding at the flat since returning to London, immediately after the shooting, telling the other tenants he was called Dave and worked for the *Evening News*. At one point he had even helped his neighbours decorate their flat while news bulletins of the police hunt appeared on television.

The trial was convened for the next sitting of the Manchester Crown Court and on 1st February, 1972, the defendants stood before Mr Justice Kilmer-Brown on a vast array of charges. The five gang members were each charged on seven counts: the murder of Superintendent Richardson; four counts of attempted murder of police officers; conspiracy that between 1st January and 23rd August, 1971, any one of them would use a firearm to prevent the arrest of any of their number; and that on 23rd August, they stole a quantity of jewellery from Joseph Lammond.

Sewell, Spry, Bond and Haynes all pleaded not guilty to the first six charges, but admitted robbery. Flannigan denied all the charges.

It was learned that the gang had visited Blackpool on the previous weekend when they made a reconnaissance of the area, and selected the best roads to use in the event of a chase. Witnesses testified how shortly before the murder they had seen the gang transfer from the gold Ford Capri to the green Triumph. All were carrying holdalls, and one witness claimed he thought one of them had placed a gun in the boot before slamming it shut.

On the second day of the trial PC Walker, one of the wounded officers, gave evidence and identified Spry as the man who had shot at him while he sat behind the wheel of his panda car. When arrested, Spry was alleged to have claimed that he had lost his memory, and held his head in his hands denying any knowledge of the two who escaped.

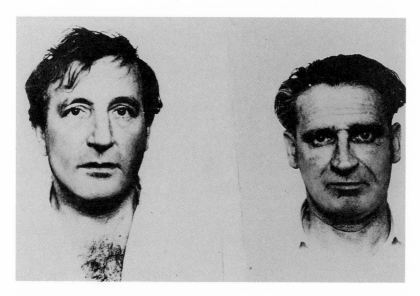

Left Bond and *right* Flannigan. *(Newspix)*

Another officer, PC Jackson, told the court that it was Sewell who had pointed a gun at him as he sat in the panda car and threatened him with, 'Get out and you're dead.'

When the defendants themselves took the stand, Flannigan claimed he was an innocent bystander who had been bundled into the car during the robbery, and had in fact been kidnapped!

'I don't care how many died,' he was alleged to have said. 'It's got . . . all to do with me.'

When Sewell stood in the dock he claimed that he had shot Superintendent Richardson by accident, and that the gun had gone off during a struggle. This was refuted by a ballistics expert, called as a prosecution witness, who claimed that the pull on the trigger was such that it would take significant pressure to fire and that the gun was unlikely to go off accidentally.

Sewell's counsel made an attempt to discredit the expert, who was appearing at his first murder trial, but with little success. They also claimed that police had doctored some of the statements, which they had bullied out of several of the witnesses. The various defence counsels offered pleas of manslaughter and unlawful wounding, alleging that most of the gang had no idea that guns were to be used.

115

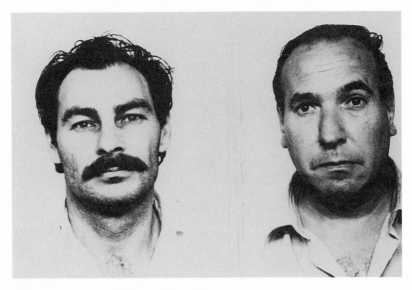

Left Haynes and *right* Spry. *(Newspix)*

The trial lasted 45 days – the same length of time as the manhunt – and ended with the jury taking just four and a half hours to find all the defendants guilty. The judge passed sentences totalling 193 years.

Sewell was found guilty of murder and sentenced to life imprisonment, with a recommendation that he serve 30 years. He also received 15 years for robbery, 20 years for attempted murder and 15 years for conspiracy to use firearms, all sentences to run concurrently. Spry received sentences totalling 75 years: 20 for manslaughter, 25 for attempted murder and 15 years for conspiracy. Again, all were to run concurrently. Bond received 15 years for robbery, as did Flannigan, while Haynes, who had driven the getaway car, was sentenced to ten years.

The exact content of their haul was later revealed in court: the men had stolen 684 rings, 117 watches, 38 bracelets, 104 charms or pendants, 53 pair of ear-rings and 71 pairs of cuff-links. The value was put at £106,033.

Sewell was sent to Gartree maximum security prison at Leicester, while the others were spread around various provincial gaols. In mid

FOR JUSTICE and LAW
GOOD MEN MUST DIE
BUT DEATH CANNOT
KILL THEIR NAMES
+
To the Beloved Memory of
GERALD IRVING
RICHARDSON. G.C.
Superintendent Lancashire Constabulary. Blackpool Division
WHO DIED IN THE PERFORMANCE OF HIS DUTY
23rd August 1971. Aged 38 Years

1974, Sewell was the ringleader in a breakout from the gaol but was arrested in a field beside the A6 and returned to prison. He was later transferred to another high security prison. With the exception of Sewell all the gang served their sentences, less remission, and were released. Sewell is still serving his sentence, having forecast to his friends that he would die in gaol.

Later that year Superintendent Gerald Irving Richardson was posthumously awarded the George Cross – the highest civil award for bravery. The Queen presented the award to his widow, Maureen, at Buckingham Palace in December. The other officers involved on that fateful day were also awarded for their bravery.

Superintendent Richardson was later awarded a 'Medal of Honor' by the American Police Federation and his name was recorded in the United States Police Hall of Fame – 'so that his sacrifice and his dedication to humanity and justice will always be remembered by generations to come.'

19

THE VENDETTA

THE MURDER OF WILLIAM OPENSHAW AT BROUGHTON, MAY 1981

Motives for premeditated murder come in many forms, with jealousy, greed and revenge high on the list. The killing of a circuit judge in the spring of 1981 was the culmination of a deep-seated hatred that took root at the beginning of 1968, when two men stood trial at the Lancashire Quarter Sessions.

Mr Justice William Openshaw was following in his father's, grandfather's and great-grandfather's footsteps when he was called to the bar in 1936, practising on the Northern circuit. Between 1958 and 1971 he was chairman of the Lancashire Quarter Sessions and Recorder of Preston and from 1972 he was made an Honorary Recorder, dealing entirely with criminal cases at the crown court. He was married and had two sons, the eldest son Peter being a practising barrister in Manchester.

At 8.20am, 12th May, 1981, Judge Openshaw kissed his wife goodbye at their large detached home, Park House, off the A6 at Broughton, and walked across the drive to the detached garage. He was due to preside over the second day of a case at the crown court at Preston, a five mile drive from his home.

The Judge reached the garage and raised the door, and as he did so he found himself face to face with a man wielding a knife. The Judge was a tall man and powerfully built for a 71 year old, but so swift was the attack that he had no time to defend himself. He gave out a cry for help as the man ruthlessly stabbed at him with the knife, delivering a dozen wounds in the thigh, chest and neck.

Joyce Openshaw had just opened the back door to take out some rubbish when she heard her husband cry out. As she approached the garden she saw the figure of a man sitting in her husband's car, which had been driven onto the drive and had the engine ticking over.

Mr Justice William Openshaw. *(Lancashire Evening Post)*

Scene of the murder. *(Peter G. Reed)*

There was no sign of her husband and fearing he could have been the target for a kidnapping, she rushed back to the house and telephoned the police. Returning to the garage, she saw the car was still there with the engine running, and walking inside the garage she found her husband lying in a pool of blood. There was no sign of the attacker. An ambulance was summoned but the Judge's injuries were so severe that he died before reaching hospital.

Superintendent Ray Rimmer, the deputy head of Lancashire CID took charge of the case and immediately ordered the use of a helicopter to swoop over the area in an attempt to find the killer, who could have gone to ground in the surrounding woodland. Police officers visited all farmers and villagers in the area asking if they had seen anyone acting suspiciously. No weapon was found at the scene and although the helicopter made several swoops across the area it brought no results. Mrs Openshaw gave detectives a description of the attacker and road blocks were ordered throughout Lancashire, looking for a dark complexioned man in his mid twenties.

Courts throughout the region were adjourned as a mark of respect

Walter George Hide. *(Peter G. Reed)*

and Rimmer's first job was to check through a number of the Judge's recent cases as it was just possible that the murder had been the result of someone carrying a grievance against him. How close this was to the truth would soon become apparent.

The hunt for the killer was not a long one. Company director George Hide of Goosnargh, near Preston, was driving north up the A6 when he was brought to a halt as a man jumped in front of the car. The man was waving furiously, and thinking there had been an accident, Hide stopped the car. The passenger door was unlocked and the man jumped into the seat and shouted 'Drive!' Holding a wicked-looking, bloodstained hunting knife, the hijacker turned to the driver and said 'Just do as I say and you won't get hurt.' They went north and joined the M6 just north of Forton services, heading for Scotland. Reaching the town of Hawick in Galloway, the hijacker turned to the driver and told him to pull over. He had apparently planned to conceal the driver in the boot of the car, but had flagged down an Austin hatchback, so he lashed the frightened man to a tree with a pair of jump leads before driving off.

Mr Hide quickly managed to free himself from his shackles and called the police. Road blocks were hastily set up and within the hour a man was under arrest. He was stopped at a road block and attempted to make off on foot, being brought to the ground by a rugby tackle from an unarmed constable. He was still carrying the murder weapon when arrested.

Later that afternoon he was identified as 32 year old John Smith of no fixed abode, but a native of Burnley where his next of kin resided. He was interviewed by Detective Chief Inspector Jeff Meadows and when the detective asked him, 'Why did you do it, John?', Smith replied, 'Because he was a bastard. He sent me down the first time on five charges; unauthorised taking, house-breaking and shop-breaking. He never gave me a chance.' The story of Smith's long quest for revenge was revealed.

Fourteen years previously, 18 year old John Smith and his partner in crime, 49 year old George Boyle had roamed the streets of Worsthorne, Burnley, in search of easy pickings, specialising in the theft and re-sale of scrap metal. One cold February night in 1968, the two had caught the bus over to nearby Nelson where they spent the night in a number of public houses. At closing time they found that the last bus had just gone. A taxi was beyond their means and rather than face the long walk home, at Smith's suggestion they had stolen a van. As a result, a few weeks later they found themselves face to face with Mr Justice Openshaw at Burnley Magistrates Court.

Smith had decided as he stood in the dock that he would make a clean break from his criminal activities, and admitted a score of other offences, mostly taking and driving away, and theft of scrap metal. After listening to the cases, Mr Justice Openshaw sentenced Boyle to 18 months' imprisonment, suggesting to the jury that he was the instigator, and had led his young friend astray. Smith was sent to Borstal for 18 months and banned from driving for a similar period.

Sitting in the cells below, waiting to be transferred to Risley remand centre, Smith seemed to have been resigned to the sentence and turned to Boyle. 'This has got to be the last time, George. I'm going to stay clean after this.' But with all his good intentions, Borstal was tough on the young offender, and as he sat in his cramped cell day after day, Smith had become a ticking time-bomb, a powder keg waiting to explode as he built up a deep hatred for the man he believed responsible for his predicament. He swore revenge, and the anger had only grown over the years, until it came to encompass not only the judge but the whole legal system.

Smith wanted to tell the world about his grudge. He had made headlines across the country the previous summer when he staged a protest at the top of Blackpool tower, earning himself the nickname in the press of 'The Birdman of Blackpool', before being persuaded down.

Asked if he had considered any other names on his hit list, Smith claimed that his first choice had been Lord Hailsham, the Lord Chancellor. He admitted travelling to London a few weeks earlier but had changed his mind when he realised that Hailsham had done him no personal harm, and decided instead to target Mr Openshaw. He had checked up on Judge Kershaw, who had also sent him down, and on top police officers McNee and Anderton. He had thought about attacking members of the Royal Family but decided they were afforded too much protection.

One man who was not on his list was the then Home Secretary William Whitelaw who had recently implemented the 'short, sharp, shock' treatment for young offenders. Smith told the detective that if he had received this type of punishment it might have worked in his case.

He concluded his interview by saying: 'Me and Openshaw are the losers; I'll now be incarcerated for the rest of my life. Who's the worst off, him or me? I'll be rotting in jail.'

Smith was remanded in custody to await trial at the Crown Court. His legal representation was handled by Mr Barrington Black who numbered among his former clients Donald Nielsen – the Black Panther and whose first action was to ask for a change in the trial venue. Black argued that because the Judge was a well known and respected figure in Lancashire, Smith could not be guaranteed a fair hearing. The trial was arranged for Leeds Crown Court in November.

On Wednesday, 18th November, 1981, John Smith was tried before Mr Justice Lawson. Entering the dock, the clerk of the court asked Smith for his name and he refused to answer. There was a lengthy debate and after 40 minutes pleas were entered on his behalf on the charges of murder, kidnapping and false imprisonment. Throughout the 40 minutes, Smith kept up a tirade of abuse at people in the court.

Flanked by three burly prison warders, Smith stood impassive in the dock as the proceedings began. His defence counsel, Mr Ivan Lawrence QC, explained that pleas of not guilty could be entered if Smith refused to answer the indictment, adding that Smith refused to plead because he recognised neither the charge against him, nor the court itself. 'On the first, he feels it should be a charge of treason, on

John Smith. *(John Lomas)*

the second he wishes to have access to the European Court of Human Rights.' He then told the judge that his client wished to take no further part in the trial and asked to be allowed to leave the courtroom. When this was refused, Smith sat on the floor with his back to the judge, and as the jury were sworn in, he again started shouting abuse and insults towards the court.

The defence rested solely on a prepared statement by Smith which was read to the court by Miss Louise Godfrey, his junior counsel. Smith claimed he would never get a fair hearing in this country because everyone in the legal profession knew the victim. 'I haven't either admitted or denied the charge,' said Smith, 'so all of you can't be 100% sure that I did what they say, even if I did.'

The evidence took up a whole day and ended when the jury returned and announced that they had found the defendant guilty, with a majority of 10 – 2. Mr Justice Lawson then sentenced Smith to life imprisonment with a recommendation that he serve a minimum of 25 years. He received a further five years for kidnapping.

Unrepentant, Smith screamed abuse as the sentence was passed and as he was hustled from the dock by four warders, he turned to the judge and shouted, 'If I ever get out, I'll cut your throat. I'm not sorry for what I have done, I would do it again if I had the chance.'

John Smith had taken 14 years to achieve his macabre desire to exact revenge on the Judge. While awaiting trial he made a statement explaining why he committed the crime. 'If he hadn't sent me down he would still be alive today, and I wouldn't be the monster that I am.' He will probably spend the rest of his days behind bars.

Index

Allen, Harry 12
Allen, Det Chief Insp
  Louis 89, 93, 95
Allen, Margaret 50-55
Allen, William O'Meara 11
Appleton, Gladys 32-37
Ardwick 9
Ashton-under-Lyne 9, 56-61
Atkinson, Mr Justice
  Fenton 192

Ball, Supt James 32, 35
Balmer, Chief Supt 74-75
Barker, George 32-33
Belle Vue 11
Birkdale 30
Birkett, Norman 19
Black, Barrington 123
Blackburn 46, 62, 63, 86-92,
  93, 95, 106, 108-117
Blackpool 12, 16, 62, 86, 123
Bolton 103, 104, 105, 106
Bond, Dennis
  George 110-117
Brett, Sergeant Charles 11
Broughton 118-125
Burke, Kenneth 37, 63-65
Burnley 98-102, 122
Burns, Alfred 75-80
Butcher, Det Insp 96, 97

Caldwell, Charlie and
  Eliza 22-24

Chadwick, Florence 98-102
Chadwick, Nancy 50-55
Clayton, Walter 47-49
Cleminson, Det Supt 40-45
  passim
Collins, Det Chief Supt
  Alfred 103-105 passim
Corbitt, James Henry 56-61
Crichton, J. Robertson 70,
  84, 91
Cross, Isabella 93-97
Cunningham, Det Chief Supt
  Eric 93-97 passim
Cusack, Mr Justice 106

Davidson, John
  Gordon 32-37
Davies, Det Supt Jim 87, 89,
  90
'Deasey, Captain' 9-11
Devlin, Edward Francis 75-80
Djorovic, Radomir 62-65

Eanam 86, 87, 95
Edenfield 62, 63

Finnimore, Mr Justice 77, 78
Firth, Dr 26
Flannigan, Thomas 110-117
Floyd, Supt 46, 48
Fyfe, Sir David Maxwell 80

Galbraith, James 43-45

Gallagher, Frederick 86-92, 93
Galvin, Mrs Gene 34, 35
Gardner, Douglas 100-102
Glaister, Professor John 16
Goddard, Lord Chief Justice 65, 78, 80
Goldie, Sir Noel 77-78
Gorman, Lord Chief Justice William 54, 97
Gould, William 11
Green, Norman William 83-85

Hagan, Mary 25-28
Harmer, Billy 81, 83, 84
Harrap, Sergeant 9
Harwood 103-107
Hayes, Charles 110-117
Helibron, Rose 17
Help the Poor Struggler pub 56
Hide, Walter George 121-122
Hilbery, Mr Justice 37, 45, 92
Hinchcliffe, Mr Justice 91
Hogg, Superintendent 46
Hucker, Mr Justice 23-24
Hunter, Det Chief Insp Ian 106

Jackson, Det Chief Supt 26, 27
Jacques, Joyce 46-49
Johnson, Det Sgt 100
Jones, Mr Justice 63
Jump, PC 9

'Kelly, Colonel' 9-11
Kenyon, Alan 103-107
Kilmer-Brown, Mr Justice 114
Kirkdale 9
Kovacevic, Nenad 62-65

Lancashire Borough Police Force, formation 8
Lancaster 9, 14-21, 91
Larkin, Michael 11
Lawrence, Mr Ivan 123-124
Lawrence, Supt Sydney 39
Lawson, Mr Justice 123, 124
Lee, Gordon Leonard 106-107
Lindsay, Det Chief Supt 57, 62-63, 69, 82
Little Hulton 66, 70
Liverpool 12, 25-28, 30, 31, 40, 49, 58, 70, 72-80, 96
Lower Ince 81-83
Lynskey, Mr Justice 58, 60

McClaughlin, George 74, 75, 76
McGinn, Det Sgt 34, 35
Maddocks, Det Insp John 32, 35
Manchester 12, 20, 23, 37, 45, 63, 65, 66, 70, 74, 75, 76, 78, 84, 93-97, 106, 114
Mather, Mona 66-71
Mercer, Chief Supt 69
Mighall, Det Insp 30
Miles Platting 93
Moffat 16
Morecambe 17, 46-49
Morgan, Samuel 27-28
Mounsey, Det Supt 113, 114

Neild, Basil 77-78
Nelson, Mr H. 70
New Bailey prison 10-11

Oliver, Mr Justice 70, 84, 85
Openshaw, William 118-125
Osliff, Imeldred 29-31

Parkinson, Det Insp   101
Peel, Sir Robert   8
Percy, James   38-45
Philpott, Det Insp   34
Pierrepoint, Albert   12, 56,
   61, 65
Platt, Chief Supt   62
Poczy, Mihaly   89-92
Police, early days   8-13
Preston   9, 26, 35, 45, 46, 89,
   91, 93, 94, 95, 105, 106,
   118, 121
Price, Inspector   46
punishments, early   9

Rawtenstall   50-55
Richardson, Supt
   Gerald   108-117
Rimmer, Beatrice   72-80
Rimmer, Supt Ray   120
Rochdale   22-24
Rogerson, Mary   14-21
Rosen, Mr   59, 61
Rossendale   62-55
Rowland, Walter   12
Ruxton, Buck and
   Isabella   14-21

St Anne's   12
St Helens   32-37
Salford   9, 11, 12, 38-45
Salmon, Mr Justice   97
Sandygate   98, 100, 101
Seaforth   27

Sewell, Frederick
   Joseph   110-117
Singleton, Mr Justice   19
Slater, Det Insp   100, 101
Smith, James   95-97
Smith, John   117-125
Southport   29-31
Spry, John Patrick   110-117
Stable, Mr Justice   49, 96
Stevens, Chief Inspector   50,
   52-54
Strangeways prison   20, 24,
   45, 55, 61, 65, 71
Stretford   43

Taylor, Supt   72
Tyldesley   66-71

Vann, Captain   18

Walton Prison   28, 31, 37, 49,
   74, 80, 85
Wavertree   72, 74
Wharton Fold   66
Whitelaw, William   123
Wigan   81-85
Woodford, Captain   8
Woodmansey, Chief Supt   46,
   50
Wooll, Edward   58
Worsthorne   122
Wright, Jack   66-71
Wrottesley, Mr Justice   31

Yates, Norman   81-85